Abou

C000184471

Sarah is the Regional General Counsel for WeWork, an international company that transforms buildings into collaborative workspaces and communities. While in her previous role as Chief Legal Officer of Kentucky Fried Chicken, she helped to steer the company successfully through the #chickencrisis of 2018, when a distribution failure led to the closure of the majority of the KFC restaurants in the UK.

Sarah has been listed on The Lawyer Hot 100 List 2019, the General Counsel Powerlist 2019 and 2016, and was the winner of the UK In-House Lawyer of the Year award in 2014. She is a sought after speaker at legal conferences around the world, and is recognised for her authenticity and courageous leadership.

Sarah serves as a trustee of the social justice charity NACRO and of the start-up charity Sal's Shoes, and is the Executive Sponsor of the 'Women of WeWork' group. She lives in Surrey with her husband, two incredibly chatty daughters, and her enormous dog, Otto.

Praise For You Didn't Mention The Piranhas

"Beautifully written, funny and insightful."
Charlie Engle, Author & Ultramarathon Runner

"It's not fair – how can a lawyer write so beautifully? Not only that, she shares her wisdom with such wit and warmth. Gift-wrapped in her own stories and scrapes, you'll find such great advice for life and work."
Neil Mullarkey, Actor, Writer & Comedian

"This book is a must read for anyone in the legal industry or in business… a brutally honest insight into the eye of the storm of a crisis, wrapped up in an authentic confessional of trying to achieve work/life balance in the law. Rarely have I read anything so honest and insightful. We often forget lawyers are human – Sarah reminds us how this should be at the heart of everything we do in the law."
David Burgess, Publishing Director, The Legal 500

"Sublime storytelling… a dazzling debut by Nelson Smith. Masterly on all levels, confidently illustrating the extraordinary side of ordinary life and filled with humour and rich observations."
CJ Bowry, Founder of Sal's Shoes

"This is a book that everyone should read at least once in their life."
Lea Korte

You Didn't Mention the Piranhas

A handbook to help you live
more bravely and successfully
navigate through any crisis

Sarah Nelson Smith

unbound

This edition first published in 2019

Unbound
6th Floor Mutual House, 70 Conduit Street, London W1S 2GF
www.unbound.com

All rights reserved

© Sarah Nelson Smith, 2019

The right of Sarah Nelson Smith to be identified as the author of this work
has been asserted in accordance with Section 77 of the Copyright, Designs
and Patents Act 1988. No part of this publication may be copied,
reproduced, stored in a retrieval system, or transmitted, in any form or by
any means without the prior permission of the publisher, nor be otherwise
circulated in any form of binding or cover other than that in which it is
published and without a similar condition being imposed on the subsequent
purchaser.

ISBN (eBook): 978-1-78965-058-7
ISBN (Paperback): 978-1-78965-057-0

Cover design by Mecob
Author photograph by Carlo Navato
Illustrated by Josh Hara

Printed and bound in Great Britain by Clays Ltd, Elcograf S.p.A.

MIX
Paper from
responsible sources
FSC   FSC® C018072

For Mattie & Jossie:

you make life more colourful just by being in it.

Contents

Introduction: The Beginning

My dad had a Canon AE-1 camera. A weighty chrome and black machine with interchangeable lenses, it was the world's first camera with an embedded microcomputer, representing the incorporation of automatic and electronic technologies with the 35mm SLR. The AE-1 was equipped with an electronically controlled, electromagnet shutter, with a speed range of 2 to 1/1000 second, and had game-changing automated functions such as automatic flash exposure control. Even if I had known any of this back in 1984, it would have meant nothing to me. All I knew was that underneath the brown leather carry case with the stiff press-stud fastening, lay a piece of equipment with more dials and buttons and moving parts than my five-year-old heart could ever dream of twisting and pulling and pressing. This camera was a thing of beauty. A thing so important that it came with its own small pink silk cloth with scalloped edges specifically for wiping away the motes of dust that managed to reach its lenses on the occasions that my dad took it out for use. This camera was not for me.

My mum tells me that I can't have been more than five when my dad stormed into the kitchen and, with barely contained fury, said that somebody had taken his camera, removed the reel and pulled out the film from within it. This same person (although, in fairness, my dad had no supporting evidence of this) had given each of the other four reels stored with it the same treatment. At a guess, I would say that such small person was merely trying to find out where all the pictures were hidden, but I digress. My mum, a barrister, correctly surmised that Dad had managed to narrow the suspects down to a pool of two: my seven-year-old sister, and myself. Due to a string of unrelated recent misdemeanours (such as collecting dozens of woodlice and storing them in the fireplace, where they bred, and bred, and bred... and experimenting with the car cigarette lighter and the tightly coiled acrylic carpeting of my dad's brand new canary yellow Ford Sierra) I was thrust, rather unfairly, into primary suspect position. 'I have no doubt,' my father said, 'that this was Sarah.'

'Well, of course there's some doubt,' my mum correctly pointed out, 'so you must ask her.'

So he did. Several minutes later, my father returned to the kitchen.

'Well?' my mum probed. 'Did you ask Sarah whether it was her?' My father, looking crestfallen, confirmed that he had. 'And?' said my mum. 'What did she say?'

My father, confused, said that I had asked him what day the films had been exposed.

'So what did you tell her?' my mum asked.

'I told her that I didn't know what day.'

'And?' my mum pressed.

'And,' my dad continued, with the air of defeat settling heavily around his shoulders, 'she said that, in that case, she couldn't know whether it had been her.'

Now firmly rooted in family folklore, this story will be lovingly embellished and enthusiastically retold by my mother to anybody who stops by for coffee. With tears of pride in her eyes, she will tell you that this was the moment when she knew, beyond doubt, that her adventurous and mischievous daughter was going to be a lawyer.

*

Not everyone is clear on the path that their future career will take at such a young age, however. Nor would such predestination appeal to all. But at some point, it suddenly hits us that the future that we've been anticipating, whether eagerly or with some trepidation, is here. The adults who once orchestrated our lives have taken a step back and, in their place, we stand, a little bewildered, perhaps, as it dawns on us that we are now expected to orchestrate both our own lives and those of the children, team members and colleagues who might play a part in them.

It may well be that you are one of life's wonderful, meticulous planners; that you take time each year or quarter to look back at your successes and analyse how each was achieved. It might be that you take ownership of each of any losses and failures, ensuring that you understand the cause of them and mapping out a plan for avoiding the same missteps in future. Perhaps you have taken stock of where you stand today, and can pinpoint where you aim to be standing tomorrow, next week or in five years' time, with a roadmap of how exactly you're going to get there.

Yet the unforeseen can ambush even such a person. Course mapped and hopes high, you set off on the right tack. But, despite all your efforts, the storm hits. Your best-laid plans dissolve to wishes as you realise that fate or destiny or Sod's Law or ill fortune by any other name has other ideas and, like flotsam, you have no option but to go with it for now.

This is a book for such moments: for reading in a leisurely

fashion whilst mapping out the course that you plan to navigate. Or, indeed, it's a book for grabbing in rather more urgent a manner, once the storm is looming large on the horizon, or even as it claws at the sails and tauntingly roars at you that nobody can out-plan a crisis!

Well, yes, you can: you might not be able to plan a path around it, but you can certainly steel yourself, grit your teeth, and plot a course right the way through it.

> In preparing for battle I have always found that plans are useless, but planning is indispensable.
> – Dwight D. Eisenhower, thirty-fourth president of the United States

Part I of this book considers different lenses of self-reflection: how much credence should you give to feedback, whether positive or negative, well-intentioned or otherwise? And how do you extract something positive from it in order to learn and grow? Having a realistic view of your strengths and weaknesses is the best platform from which to enhance one and reduce the other, so Part I of this book will help you to recognise which feedback and guidance will enable you to do this. It also explores how to assess correctly which of life's challenges are to be avoided like the plague, and which should be seized and bravely faced head-on, no matter how shaky the hand that seizes them.

Part II looks at the role you're in and the people, or tribe, with which you choose to surround yourself. Once you're sure that both are as you'd want or need them to be, this part turns to the necessity of taking the time to fully understand the situation that you're in. Here, the Kentucky Fried Chicken distribution crisis of 2018 is used as a key example, and the background to a very public failure is explored.

By Part III, the time for horizon-scanning and wondering whether disaster might be avoided has passed. The proverbial s*** has hit the fan, and you are left standing there, trying to figure out how on earth to clear it all up again. This part shares thoughts on how to recognise, as early as possible, that all is not as it should be (it might sound obvious, but there are many examples in business and in life generally of salvageable situations rapidly worsening, simply because nobody has acknowledged that anything is amiss). From the epicentre of the storm, what steps can you take to navigate through to calm waters again, and in a way that occasions the least-lasting damage to things, to relationships, to your own physical and mental health?

All things pass. Soon, the crisis will be behind you, but the journey will not yet be complete: what can be learned from all that has happened? The landscape may look very different now and you might be unwise to assume that whatever was right for you before will still be the correct solution now. Part IV of this book explores how and when to walk away from the situation with hard-won insights and a clear vision of the new path ahead.

Throughout this book, there are tips and tools to help you put the ideas that it raises into practice, and references to people far wiser than me who have considered and learned from their own set of challenges. As and when time permits, you can read *You Didn't Mention the Piranhas* from cover to cover: the equivalent of a long conversation between the two of us over a bottle of wine (or two), and a decent selection of bar snacks. Or you can flick through its pages and hone in on the topics that you're grappling with at the moment: the literary equivalent of a quick WhatsApp exchange:

Reader: *!!!!!!!!!!!!*

Sarah: *What's up?*

Reader: *Total nightmare!! I'd hoped we were going to be okay, but EXACTLY what I feared might happen is happening now! There's no chance that I'll get through this without getting fired or completely losing it!*

Sarah: *Sounds hideous! You know you can get through it, though. No doubt in my mind…*

Reader: *Well, there's a LOT of doubt in mine at the moment…*

Sarah: *Hold on – have you tried approaching it like this…*

Part I
Who are you really?

1. Figuring It Out

My head of sixth form anchored herself at the front of the lecture theatre, her woollen-stockinged legs planted wide enough apart to ensure that the tide of teenage stares had no destabilising effect on her confident, be-tweeded frame. 'You,' she proclaimed, looking each of the eighty teenage girls squarely in the eye, 'entered this school an unholy rabble of ugly ducklings.'

A rousing speech followed. We had developed and grown; learned and flourished; made mistakes and picked ourselves up and recovered from them, emerging stronger young women as a result. In the back of my mind, the inspiring words from John Irving's novel *The Cider House Rules* spooled: '... you princes of Maine, you kings of New England.'

We waited eagerly for the inevitable close to Mrs Casebourne's words: '*And now, here sits before me a beautiful bevy of swans...*' Only, they didn't come. Instead, she implored us to ensure that our lockers were emptied carefully, as it was the last day of term, and the very last thing that next year's sixth formers needed was potent three-month-old sandwiches festering in their newly allocated lockers. The lecture theatre disgorged itself of girls, heady with hope and possibility and the first delicious taste of freedom. And suddenly, my school life was behind me, leaving me with what I knew would be a life-long love of learning, deep-rooted friendships, experiences that forever shaped my character, and a lingering doubt: was I in fact still an unreformed ugly duckling?

PIECING TOGETHER THE PUZZLE
OF WHO WE ARE

The saying 'feedback is a gift' has always made me laugh: to English speakers, it has one meaning; to Germans, for whom the word 'gift' translates as 'poison', it has quite another. Perhaps both are true. This chapter looks at the various sources of, and motivations for, giving feedback. It suggests how to identify and absorb the gift, whilst eschewing the poison.

My journey always seemed to be a bit of a jigsaw puzzle to me. Right back in 1984, my mother had managed to find the pieces that slotted together to depict a future legal career. But there were still a great number of pieces yet to pick up, examine, and place carefully in a position that made sense. Finding the corner pieces was relatively easy: to function at my best, I have always needed the comfort and joy of strong friendships, the stretch that creative and intellectual challenge affords me, a good level of physical fitness that I can maintain and enjoy day to day, and also time on my own to recalibrate and make sense of my jumbled thoughts and feelings. As corner-pieces to my own jigsaw, these were pretty easy to make out.

But as to the edges – those long stretches that set the boundaries of who and what I truly understand myself to be, which contain the promise that the full picture is held within them... Could I really be sure what my boundaries were?

Having an opinion on an untested objective set of principles is easy. I remember being entirely certain that if a boyfriend cheated on me, I would obviously leave him. I had self-respect and I deserved better than that, and, if I were entirely frank, I thought people who put up with that sort of disrespectful behaviour had only themselves to blame for the repeat offences that would inevitably occur. Then my boyfriend returned from a ski holiday with friends. And, for some reason, he couldn't bring himself to look me in the eye. And when all of the sordid facts of the trip came out, I was furious and devastated and all-consumed with the hideousness of the situation, until I realised one day, a few weeks later, that, no matter how much we discussed it and how angry I was and how repentant he was, the simple facts could not change: the only thing that *could* change was my attitude to the situation. I could choose to accept it as a small and messy part of one chapter of our relationship, or I could walk away.

Both options were entirely possible, but I could only choose one, and choosing one but complaining about it would be emotionally exhausting for both of us. So I accepted what had happened, forgave him, and moved on. And life went on, and the world quietly tipped back onto its proper axis, and neither of us was thwacked between the eyes by a vengeful moral compass. Instead, we married. We built a life and a family together.

Looking back now, it's striking quite how incredibly unimportant that episode was. With the benefit of experience and perspective, there are many things that truly do not matter, and a cluster of things that really do. The challenge is knowing how to separate one from the other.

DOES YOUR OPINION MATTER TO ME?

So how to make sense of the jumble of jigsaw pieces that somehow make up the full picture of you: a riot of different shapes and colours and images? At first, there might seem to be little more than a promise that they will somehow sit harmoniously together. And, piece by piece, they do. Over time, order can eventually be born from chaos, and calm clarity from doubt and confusion. And as more of the picture is completed, so the gaps become easier and easier to fill. The true home for the missing pieces suddenly seems an easy find, when, only a few moments ago, it was impossible even to guess at what should sit where. This process of understanding yourself can, however, also be a long one (I wrote 'an arduous one' initially, but changed it: the effort is a large part of the fun). There are a number of pointers to help along the way.

Our first understanding of who we are, is of who others tell us we are. The opinion of well-meaning bystanders is at once a gift and a burden. Now that I have my own daughters, I realise more than ever the importance of carefully considering how I share with them my perceptions of them. Do I want to tell them that I think they are beautiful (and of course I believe that they are), or would that give them the impression that superficial beauty is an important benchmark by which I, and therefore the world, will judge them? And will this in turn encourage them to seek friendship with people who excel in the area I've signalled to them is important: superficial beauty? Whilst I don't want them to feel ugly, I'd rather they draw their feelings of self-worth from more fundamental and less transient characteristics. I tell them how much I love their kindness and their thoughtfulness, the fact that they seek out children at school who seem lonely and invite them to join in with their games. I praise their strong bodies, and say how grateful I feel that they're able to use them to run fast, climb high and, with courage, seek out new adventures. Of course, I also regularly point out (often fairly loudly...) how much their bickering over nothing drives me crazy, and how I wish they'd seek out a good book for entertainment more frequently than they seek out a good film, but there is work still to be done here.

As children, it's hard for them to separate out the opinions that are altruistically given, and that they should care about and take seriously, from those that they should brush aside and largely ignore. As adults, it's still difficult.

I remember standing at a cashpoint a few years ago. I was meeting up with friends for an evening out, and was dressed up, albeit with no make-up on: I never really wear any. Next to the cashpoint, a drunk man sat on the pavement, jacket slung across his knees, an open can of lager in his hand, and a suspicious pool of liquid encircling him. He heaved his head upwards and performed a slow and silent up and down appraisal of my appearance. 'You look all right, darlin',' he concluded, taking another swig, 'but you'd look a lot better with some slap on.' At the time, I remember thinking, how astute! Notwithstanding the obvious impediment of prolonged intoxication, this gentleman has accurately identified a key and fundamental flaw in the way that I look. I must... Then, thankfully, I quickly progressed to realising that here was a man, sitting in a pool of his own urine, casting judgement on whether I wore mascara and lipstick. Whilst he may well have been right, his was not an opinion that I'd lose any sleep over. He did not know me, and it truly did not matter to me what he thought.

There are numerous less stark examples. The colleague with whose opinions and morals you fundamentally disagree criticises you. Do you respect their judgement? Do you care what they think? Do you have any interest in winning their approval? Whenever somebody offers their unsolicited opinion, I always think of a scene in the play *As You Like It*. Jaques and Orlando are discussing Orlando's new love, Rosalind, when Jaques comments that he does not like her name. Orlando replies: 'There was no thought of pleasing you when she was christened.'[1] An excellent Shakespearean example of consciously not caring!

LISTENING TO OTHERS WHEN IT COUNTS

At the same time, it would be a mistake to overlook the insights that those closest to you can offer. Your family and close colleagues probably see your face more often than you do yourself, and may be more adept at reading it than you are.

When it comes to it, even complete strangers can sometimes offer a more truthful and sympathetic portrait of us than we would ourselves. I found it fascinating to watch a 'Real Beauty Sketches' exercise conducted on behalf of Dove (the toiletries and personal care brand owned by Unilever). An FBI-trained forensic artist was asked to interview women hidden behind a curtain, and draw a portrait of each of them based on her description of herself. A stranger who had just met each woman was then asked to describe the same woman to the artist, to see how their description would differ. Each pair of portraits differed enormously. The one based on the stranger's portrayal was kinder, more beautiful, happier. It was also more accurate.

According to Dove, more than half of women globally agree that when it comes to how they look, they're their own worst critic.[2] Our perception of ourselves is often far less positive than it should be, possibly because of all the unconstructive thoughts and nagging doubts that flourish in our own minds but which are thankfully filtered out (in large part) before they make it through to our mouths. Others hear only the sanitised version of our consciousness, which is generally a lot more palatable than the unedited version. But some close friends and family get the full draft text, with scribbles in the margins and plenty of crossing out and underlining. And despite our numerous imperfections, we are still loved. Perhaps seeing the flaws and scars in others can serve to reassure each of us that, actually, we're not so bad either, and that we're all only human at the end of the day.

CONSIDERING ALL THE PIECES OF THE PUZZLE

I work in an open-plan office. I have a lot of pretty fantastic colleagues whom I love to see and spend time with, yet at the end of the working day, it can feel as though I've had a sensory overload: the questions and conversations, whether I've been asking or answering or not involved at all, can fill my head and leave me longing for a moment of quiet. I sometimes stagger out of the office building, exhausted, feeling as though I've used up all but the energy required to somehow get myself home and to my front door.

But behind that front door is a family who haven't seen me all day, and who are excited to tell me and show me what they've been doing, and who want my full, enthusiastic and undivided attention. A perfect person would probably dig into their reserves of resilience and, with genuine gusto, leap into the home and play with the dog and assess the cartwheels and the paintings and suggest baking shortbread, then read stories at bedtime and possibly do a spot of light dusting before seductively suggesting an early night. For me, this is rare (indeed 'rare' slightly overstates it).

So on the days when I make it home, and have no patience with the children and go through the motions, wishing that I could fast forward and run a hot bath and switch off completely, should I feel like I've failed?

When this happened not so long ago, I sat with my eldest daughter and told her about my day. We talked about the good things and the challenging things, and the fact that I felt so tired that I didn't have the patience that I should have had, and that me getting cross with her was not fair, and was not her fault at all. And perhaps surprisingly, rather than agreeing that yes, I'm a hopeless mother and that juggling career and family is a losing battle, Mattie felt proud to be having a grown-up conversation with me about it. She appreciated the insights into adults' weaknesses, and became more open to talking about the things that she found tough to handle.

I don't know whether my pedestal has been quietly dismantled, but I rather hope it has: I want her to see me as an imperfect mother, who makes mistakes but who is open to discussing them and apologising for them and learning from them. And I want her to know that I fully expect her to make mistakes, and to have weaknesses, and that they are all simply a part of what makes her wonderfully, uniquely her.

WHAT IS THE LENS THROUGH WHICH ADVICE IS GIVEN?

I used to work with an incredible lady: Kim (not her real name) was bright and good at her job, but her emotional intelligence was off the bottom of the scale. She had absolutely no consideration for the impact that her words and behaviour might have on others. I loved working with her. Not because she was pleasant to work with – quite the contrary – but I considered myself fortunate to be able to have the opportunity to try to understand and establish a functioning relationship with somebody so closed-minded and negative and so very unlike anybody I'd met before.

In fairness, it was easy to view the situation as a personal challenge and not as an impediment, because Kim had no impact at all on me or my role. For those who worked under her management, however, it was a tougher gig. One junior man in her team, Louis, came in one day, brimming with excitement, and announced that his girlfriend had just accepted his marriage proposal! There was a big family gathering planned for the end of the year in California, and they'd decided to marry then so that everyone they cared about could be there. Through the buzz of congratulations and happy hubbub, came Kim's commanding voice: 'Don't even think of asking for time off for this! You're given too much holiday as it is. And a honeymoon is out of the question.'

Did this comment matter to Louis? Possibly, if he thought that he genuinely wouldn't be permitted annual leave for the occasion. Thinking rationally, though, he would have known that his boss's view was not the company's view, so could easily be overruled if necessary. The most glaringly obvious point to me, however, was that Kim's comment had nothing at all to do with Louis. Certainly, it was directed at him, and it sought to impact him, but in his four minutes of being in the office that day, Louis couldn't possibly have done anything to incite such a negative response. Kim was simply an angry, bitter woman. There were personal reasons for this, of course, and she no doubt had many redeeming features, but the way that she unleashed bitterness and cruelty on anyone she had some power or control over was a personal character flaw, and was no reflection on her victim.

Recognising the lens through which advice, criticism or opinion is given is key to assessing how to process it appropriately. The person who shouts that you're a ****ing **** when you take the last parking space that you were both heading towards: do they know you well enough to be able to make that call? Or are they simply angry and disappointed at the situation? Undoubtedly the latter. Whether people are speaking through their own fear and defensiveness, or jealousy, or avarice, this destructive lens distorts their comments, making their remarks at best worthless and, at worst, harmful. But it's our own choice what we do with that advice. Whether to pick through the shards looking for the grains of truth that might be amongst them, or simply to dispose of the whole lot and think no more about it. There's no 'correct' answer. The only incorrect answer, though, would be to accept the poisoned apple of distorted advice and hungrily devour it as an accurate personal judgement, inviting the resultant negative impact that it will have on you. Don't allow this.

DO YOU SHARE MY VALUES?

For various obscure reasons, during my long university holidays in the summer of 2001, I booked a one-way ticket to Phoenix, Arizona. I had plans to travel through Mexico, Belize and Guatemala with a couple of friends, and pick up a flight from Guatemala City back to London, via Detroit, leaving on 11 September (although, for obvious reasons, the return did not go as planned). I had never been to America before, and I had no idea where to stay in Phoenix. I'm not sure that I'd even got as far as buying a Lonely Planet guide – my usual travel staple – so we stepped off the plane and decided to ask a taxi driver, first, where he'd recommend that we stay, and, second, to take us there. All went to plan. And we headed to the YMCA, Phoenix.

In hindsight, perhaps I should have asked the taxi driver where he himself likes to stay when he travels, or what he would look for in a good hotel. Because I'd be very surprised if the attributes of the YMCA, Phoenix would have featured on my list had I completed the same exercise. Whilst there was no spa, no organic miniature toiletries and no delicious but calorific breakfast buffet, there was (i) a security policy that strictly forbade men and women to occupy the same floor (when the lift doors closed on my friend John, taking him away from us on the third floor, up to a men-only floor on the fourth, I saw real fear in his eyes); (ii) a communal lounge room on each level (although we were warned in no uncertain terms by a fellow third-floor female resident *not* to sit on the sofas, because 'some of the ladies here, they like to urinate on them...'); and (iii) a lock-down policy at night, for the safety and security of all of the residents.

Whilst spending a night in the YMCA, Phoenix was not, in itself, particularly impactful (possibly due to the excellent security and the advice regarding the sofas that I heeded absolutely), the real value in my stay there was the lesson that the episode taught me: our viewpoints differ enormously and should be handled accordingly.

Be selective

Whilst advice and guidance can be well intentioned and honestly given, if the advisor has an entirely different outlook on life, beware of accepting it wholeheartedly as a rule to be cut and pasted into your own life.

Interrogate it, understand it, and then decide for yourself how applicable it really is for your circumstances, and what credence, if any, to give it.

CARE, BUT NOT TOO MUCH

I have always loved the Serenity Prayer, written by the American theologian Reinhold Niebuhr:

> God, grant me the serenity to accept the things I cannot change,
> Courage to change the things I can,
> And wisdom to know the difference.

Whether willing God to grant us these virtues, or simply willing ourselves to discover them in us, this message rings true for me. It reminds me to let go and not feel stressed in a traffic jam: either I'll get there on time, or I won't, but my state of mind in this car right now will have absolutely no impact on the eventual outcome – so why not choose to remain sanguine? It also reminds me to receive constructive personal feedback, and act on it where appropriate, but to remember that I am still human, and I am therefore still flawed and weak at times. Even if my bar is set at perfection, it's actually okay not to reach that bar.

From 2011 to 2018, I worked for Kentucky Fried Chicken

in the European Legal Team. We had a KFC bucket that sat on the desk, just next to the emergency chocolate box. Reading the bucket from a certain position, the letters 'KFC' read 'FCK' (a premonition of things to come perhaps). This was our 'f**k it bucket'. Some situations, some comments, despite our best efforts, cannot be changed for the better, and simply are what they are. These can either hang heavy on our minds and distract us while we make continued futile attempts to ameliorate them, or we can encourage each other to write the trouble down on a scrap of paper and chuck it in the f**k it bucket. I generally favoured the latter.

DECIDE WHO YOU WANT TO BE

I have always loved sports. Whether it's mountain biking, snowboarding, horse riding, swimming, tennis, golf or anything else I've had a go at, I feel at my best when I'm stuck into a decent routine of regular exercise. When I fall out of that routine, though, it can be a challenge to get back into it. Moving house several years ago meant I couldn't stop off at the local pool which sat very handily across the road from my old house for an hour's swim first thing in the morning, and, unless unpacking boxes and assembling furniture counted, I hadn't managed to find a replacement sporting activity. The psychological (as well as practical) hurdle of finding a new routine that would work for me, which I'd both enjoy and would stick at, stopped me from starting any new activity at all. I could go running, but where would I run? I could try the pool at the local leisure centre, but I have always found huge and unfamiliar swimming pools intimidating. The reason is simply that, as a child, I found swimming hard. My rounded frame was not built to float, so being made to practise lifesaving whilst wearing pyjamas and diving for bricks sent me into a blind panic.

Ever since then, whilst I love outdoor swimming, the smell of chlorine makes my heart race, and going to a huge public pool that I'm not familiar with is a very unpleasant experience for me.

One warm, sunny Friday after work, instead of heading straight home, I changed, pulled on my trainers, and just ran. I explored the town, following paths and ginnels, discovering parks and playgrounds. I paused to do pull-ups on the monkey bars and box jumps on the climbing frame, simply because they were there and I was there and life was good. As I ran towards the lake, past a brace of ducks too lazy to be startled into flight, I spotted a group of runners heading towards me. About ten men and women, several sporting race 'finisher' tops, powered across the distance between us significantly more swiftly than the progress I made toward them. This was a team of sports people, and I was simply a pretender, having put my trainers on that day for the first time in weeks. But, as the group passed me, each one smiled and nodded, acknowledging me as one of them. They saw me as a runner! I've no doubt it sounds ridiculous, but that immediate acceptance and acknowledgement felt empowering, and addictive. It made the new possibility of running tangible and real. Years later, I read the words of John Bingham, the American marathon runner who inspired many to simply begin, and I agreed with his sentiment completely:

If you run, you are a runner. It doesn't matter how fast or how far. It doesn't matter if today is your first day or if you've been running for twenty years. There is no test to pass, no license to earn, no membership card to get. You just run.

It goes without saying, but I'll say it anyway: this applies in all other areas of life. You've always wanted to play an instrument?

Learn one! You've always wanted to be patient? Take a breath and try simply being the person that you've hoped to be.

Helen, my messiest of friends, realised a few years ago that she was not prepared to be the woman who was too exhausted at the end of the day to care about what she or her home looked like, and who accepted that life was simply chaotic, with no meaningful time for herself. So she stopped being that person. Instead, she deep-cleaned her home, ridding it of all of the junk that cluttered her shelves and floor space and mind, and she changed her attitude: slumping on the sofa each evening didn't really give her energy or any feeling of satisfaction. Instead, she took up yoga (a cliché? Perhaps, but clichés are clichés for a reason), changed her diet and sleep patterns and, with the exception of her incredible personality which has never wavered, she has become the person that she'd always admired and wanted to be, simply by having the courage to admit to herself that it was possible.

One of the many fantastic things about being human is that we have the freedom and the ability to reinvent ourselves whenever we choose. There are some obvious points at which to do so: I have a friend who quit smoking and took up exercise the week before starting a new job. For years, she was the most stalwart member of the group of smokers who would cluster on the back steps of the office at regular intervals throughout the day, but she began to feel hemmed in by her own reputation. She exercised very little and felt pretty unhealthy, yet hated the fact that she was perceived by others as being unhealthy. She believed that if her new colleagues met her as an exercise junkie and a definite non-smoker, the habits that she formed around this new persona would help her to maintain it. The 'fake it till you make it' theory worked: her routines became reality, and she has never looked back.

CHOOSE HAPPINESS

It's so easy to create barriers and hurdles for ourselves when in fact none exist, or none need to exist. So many of us tell ourselves that we'll feel a certain way only when a particular milestone is reached: *I know I'll be truly happy once I've lost the extra weight / changed jobs / moved house / cleared out my wardrobe...* Whatever it is, this way of thinking is pointless. People much heavier than you, and with far messier houses than you, are happy today. And many slim, aesthetically impeccable humans living in houses that seem ready for an *Ideal Home* photo shoot are entirely miserable. The mistake is to believe that our surroundings or other such details can truly change or reverse our state of mind. As Tolstoy advised, 'If you want to be happy, be.' Happiness can be a choice.

Clearly some things make it harder for us to find true contentment and peace of mind, but separating the circumstantial and the mental state is also possible. If it just so happens that many of the components of your life are not as you'd want them to be, and potentially it's out of your control to change them, the one element that you *can* control is your mind-set. If you have no option right now but to be in a stage of life that you simply can't wait to see the back of, you can choose to make it worse by allowing yourself to dwell on the utter misery of your situation. Or, you can choose happy.

Of course, it sounds glib and facile to say that regardless of what is going on you can simply choose to be happy. But I believe that, more often than not, you can. It's sometimes an uncomfortable choice.

My dad died when I was seventeen. He had had cancer for a year, and in the last few months, he was suffering horribly. My mum seemed to suffer just as much. She cared for him around the clock, all the while watching the colour and the life draining out of the man she had known and loved for all of her adult life. His breathing rasped. Speech was laboured and painful. Life hurt in every way possible, yet at the same time was impossibly precious as it was so evidently nearly at an end. There was nothing at all to be happy about. And yet.

I'd come home from school, head straight for his bedroom, and climb into bed with him and tell him every last detail about my day. The crazy minutiae that matter immensely to a teenager but which are beyond boring to most sane adults had become a bright distraction to my dad's quiet and sombre hours in bed. He would laugh until it hurt, not caring about the pain this time. And when he was too tired to laugh, he'd sit and smile at the stories. To a teenage girl, having your father's undivided attention and love is a gift that, no matter the circumstances of its being given, is something to treasure. I read poetry to him, and stories that I'd heard, or that I'd written, and for those hours that we spent together, I was happy. Was he happy too? I choose to believe so.

With any situation, whether entering into it or emerging from it, be intentional about how you choose to feel about it. Having a positive mind-set is always an option available to you.

KEYS TO FIGURING IT OUT

- Understand who you are: it's not always an easy question to answer, and the answer can change and develop again and again over time, but it's important to have a good idea of what the answer is for you today. Take a long walk with the dog or spend a quiet weekend, and force yourself to answer questions that you perhaps haven't taken the time to really think about, such as: what really makes me happy? What motivates me? If I removed all the things from my life that don't add something positive to it, what would remain? And where are the gaps, where something is missing? What do I need to feel whole?

- Seek the thoughts and guidance of others to help you get a better understanding of what really makes you tick, and how you are perceived by others. But remember, not everybody's opinion carries equal weight. Some should not matter to you in the slightest. If your advisor does not share your values, the fantastic insights that successfully bring them happiness might bring you heartache.

- Understand the lens through which feedback is given to you: a lens of love is clarifying. A lens of jealousy or bitterness is distorting, at best, or entirely obscuring at worst.

- Care, but not too much: we can all try our best, but, sometimes, we won't have the reserves to do so. And sometimes even our best is not enough. That's okay too: we're human. We're imperfect. We fail. That's just life sometimes.

- Decide who you want to be. What if you dare to dream of yourself as that person? And what if you have the courage to make it happen? What might be possible then?

2. Understanding Your Comfort Zone

Your comfort zone is your psychological safe space, where you know that everything you need is within your grasp and control. In your comfort zone, there's no stress or anxiety, and no demands are heaped upon you that you can't easily meet. For some, an existence in this arena seems ideal. Living within your comfort zone is the equivalent of staying in your pyjamas all day and curling up under the duvet to watch box sets: an indulgent treat if you're in need of rest or recovery, whether mental or physical. But do it every day, and you'll quickly become bored and lazy.

Living all the time within your comfort zone means not going for that job or promotion, or putting off returning to work post-career break, because you might not achieve it, or you might not be good enough. It is not volunteering to give that presentation to a wider group than you've ever presented to, or to take on that project which is a little bigger than anything you've attempted previously. It's not signing up for that 10km run because you've never run that far before. It's not booking the holiday as you have nobody to travel with, because you might feel lonely, and people might think you odd. It's not getting up to dance to a song that you love, because people might laugh at your lack of rhythm. It's not turning up on your own to the social group, because you might not find anyone to chat with, and even if you do, you might not have anything interesting to say. It is recognising your own fear, and permitting it to dictate to you what you are capable of, allowing it to stop you from growing and becoming capable of more.

Recognise your comfort zone, and recognise the joy of stepping boldly out of it. It will always be there, to bring replenishment and peace as part of the equilibrium of a balanced life. As a well-stocked first-aid box sits ready and waiting on the shelf, however, plan not to rely on it too often.

REMEMBERING OUR OWN NEEDS

After our second daughter was born, life took on a new rhythm. This new beat was different to the terrifying yet magical early days of our first-born's arrival. Then, I was torn between a heady sense of wonder that it was possible for such a perfect creature to have been entrusted to my keeping, and asking myself what the heck I was going to do when next she woke up and cried: could she possibly be hungry again? Tired again? Needing her nappy changed again? Now, with the arrival of our second child, I was confident that we could rear her to the age of two at least (we had experience thus far), at which point she'd have a good enough grasp of English to be able to alert us to our shortcomings and any failure to feed, clothe or otherwise treat her appropriately. What I had yet to accomplish, though, was to balance the wellbeing of our exuberant two-year-old, our precious newborn, my exhausted and slightly shell-shocked husband, and myself.

Whenever I left the house, I had a bag sufficiently capacious to convey plasters, a bottle, two small changes of clothes, a teeny pot of grapes, a colouring-in book, special cuddly cow and assorted other obvious essentials, which would ensure that the needs of the younger two members of the family would be met, and all largely foreseeable disasters successfully warded off. And if they were happy, surely I would be happy too.

One hazy day in early summer, we'd planned to spend the afternoon with my mum. Arriving at our home and kicking her shoes off, she flicked on the coffee machine, gathered up my eldest into a bear hug and asked me what I'd like to do. And then it struck me: I had no clue. I knew when the baby would next want to sleep and feed, and I knew that the toddler would be delighted with anything that involved water or climbing or animals or ice cream or ideally a combination of several of the above. And I knew that my husband would love a bike ride or a pub lunch, or quiet time on his own to sleep or watch sport on TV. But me? I couldn't decipher whether I wanted company or solitude; rest or excitement (probably rest); familiarity or new experiences.

The realisation that I was so divorced from understanding my own needs was sobering. Of course, it's normal for women with new babies to lose themselves in the needs of their infant: without this, the human race might well have petered out generations ago as mothers chose a good night's sleep, a massage and then an evening out with friends over broken nights, endless nappies and mastitis; but at some point, we all need to remember who we are, and what we need to enable us to feel whole.

Being so focused on meeting the demands placed upon us that we don't simply fail to meet our own needs, but fail even to remember that we have them, is not solely the domain of new mothers. The Monday 6.31am to London Bridge is crammed with adults who were once children with limitless energy and myriad after school plans revolving around their den, the skateboard park, the local pool, the clubhouse, the place that made them feel happy and whole. And now? Do they all have such clarity about what will make them feel truly happy and contented, beyond simply another hour in bed and a holiday on the not too distant horizon?

Listen to a child or a teenager, and you'll be left in no doubt at all that they know what they want, and where the boundaries of their comfort zones are drawn: they'll have certainty that they can leap with abandon from the first and the middle diving boards, but that the top one is both prohibitively terrifying and forbidden by mum. Children have yet to master the juggling act of keeping the requirements of others ahead of or alongside their own; prioritising what is needed over what is wanted; and at the same time creating and maintaining (rather than merely occupying) a base position of comfort and security from which to operate. It's a challenging balance and one which, even after the catapult into adulthood, oscillates incessantly between success and failure.

As adults, how frequently do we take the time to review our changing needs in order to respond to them rather than simply urging ourselves on, ignoring the fact that we might be feeling exhausted or stressed or have been too far out, for too long, of our comfort zone? How often do we actively create an environment of comfort and security when we need it?

GET YOUR HYGGE ON

The Danish word *hygge* (pronounced hue-guh, not he-gee) describes a feeling or moment when everything seems to have slotted into its correct place, and life feels good. Defined as 'a pleasant and highly valued everyday experience of safety, equality, personal wholeness and a spontaneous social flow',[1] implicit in hygge is the ability to not just be present, but to recognise and enjoy the present. This could be while out sharing a good wine and great conversation with close friends, or turning your rushed evening shower into a mini-spa moment by lighting a candle, dimming the lights and keeping the family at bay behind a quietly locked door; hygge simply requires a conscious appreciation of the joy to be found in the moment. The Danes acknowledge and cherish simple rituals that are created without effort, turning life from a monotonous repetition of tasks and events into an art form.[2]

A true hygge experience can be different for everyone. For me, it is relaxing in the bath with a good book and a glass of wine after a long run. Or sinking into an oversized armchair on holiday in a little stone cottage on the Dorset coast with hot milky coffee in my favourite mug. The white-painted walls and the sloping wooden floorboards well-trod by people for hundreds of years give a calm feeling of being happily insignificant in the world's grand scheme. Hundreds before me may have sat like that, thought like that, and of them not even dust remains. There is a joy in knowing that, no matter how important you consider yourself to be, a little wonky stone cottage has been here for many more years than you have, and will remain long after you are gone.

PERFECT MOMENT

Some years before I became aware of the concept of hygge, I worked as a holiday rep in the Northern Greek region of Halkidiki. My days began early with airport runs to collect the pale new holiday makers who stood wilting in arrivals, delivering welcome presentations to fill them in on all of the adventures that lay in wait for them in the local area (some wonderful, some less so), and a frenetic schedule of visits, Q&A, preparing and delivering information packs and completing accounts and paperwork, before returning to the airport in the small hours of the following morning, with a coach full of different, brown and red holiday makers making their way back to Britain. In amongst the daily mayhem, itself scope for a book all of its own, I would try to steal a few moments to myself when I could slip down to the beach, away from the hotels and the people and the questions – and simply be. As the summer season wore on, my duties felt increasingly familiar, and I'd complete them efficiently, leaving me a few more precious moments to enjoy.

Looking at my watch one sweltering afternoon, I saw that I had three glorious hours to myself. Pulling on a pair of shorts and a top, I headed directly for the beach, and splashed north along the coast through the gentle surf. The beach umbrellas and the sun loungers gradually petered out and, in their place, only the occasional cluster of fallen rocks disrupted my route. Sandals in hand, I clambered over each obstacle, dropping down on the other side. The distance between me and the last people I'd spotted grew. My skin was sweaty and gritty from the repeated sandy climbs and the fast walk in the afternoon sun. With nobody in sight, I stripped off my clothes, leaving them in a small pile on the sand, and dived gratefully beneath the water's surface. The relief of the cool salt water on my hot shoulders took my breath away, and the ache in my back after weeks of long days and nights with little rest eased as I swam powerfully away from the shore. Finally out of breath, I turned and looked back at the place I'd come from.

The cove nestled like a secret beneath the lush green hills rising behind, while the hotels built further along the coast looked insignificant in the distance, bleached white in the glare of the sun. I was completely alone, in crystal clear water, with nothing pressing that I needed to do, nowhere I needed to be. The sweet, hot smell of an Aegean summer mingled with the salt water, and I knew beyond doubt that, right then, the moment simply could not be improved upon.

I've thought back to it frequently, trying to unpick what made it so perfect. The feeling of complete blissful relaxation wouldn't have been so special if it weren't for the fact that I'd been working so hard in the lead up to it. I needed the tranquillity, and I knew that I'd earned it. Having suffered with terrible back pain for years, feeling pain-free was something that I simply never took for granted. And being outside in the sunshine, caressed by the lull of the water in the heat of summer: even then, I knew that the deep sense of wellbeing and freedom that the moment gave me was something rare and precious.

HONING MY HYGGE

The idea of hygge, or of a moment where everything is in perfect balance is different, and personal for everyone. What makes one person feel cosy makes another claustrophobic. For me, here's what works:

- *Effort or exertion:* whether sporting, personal or work, I need to feel that I've earned the moments of calm contentment that follow.

- *Fresh water:* swimming or bathing in it, running through or alongside it or sailing on it, it makes me feel peaceful.

- *Safety:* knowing that I am in a safe and secure place.

- *No time pressures:* relief from the burden of the expectations of others, and knowing that I won't need to clock watch before racing off somewhere else.

- *Space:* I love company and socialising but I feel more relaxed when I have time to simply be, without needing to talk or to listen; when I can switch off external factors and get perspective.

What might it mean for you? What is it that you really need?

Find your comfort zone

Take time to understand what it is that you need to make you feel that all is as it should be. Do you need to run or rest? Be with friends or be alone? Have time for silent reflection or time to discuss and share ideas with others whose input you value?

Understand your comfort zone needs well now, so that, when you really need to meet them, you'll know what it is that you're looking for.

WORKING OUT: TWO DIRTY WORDS?

I was hit by a car when I was thirteen. I'd been cycling home from my grandma's house, and a terribly apologetic gentleman in a Mercedes pulled out of a side road. 'I didn't see you!' he repeated as an incantation, while the twisted frame of my bicycle protruded from underneath his front wheels, and I lay a little distance in front of it. At the time, it actually didn't seem that bad. As soon as I'd felt the nudge of his front bumper against my calf, I threw myself off my bicycle and as far away from the vehicle as I could, so whilst I was cut and knocked and bruised, I came off infinitely better than the bike that lay beneath his car.

The cuts and grazes healed, and a new bike arrived, but the

damage done to my spine that day plagued me for the coming decades. I might go for weeks or months without any problems at all, but then my hips would start to seize up, and then my lower back, and soon I'd be crippled by pain if I so much as breathed deeply. Having a cold when my back was bad was terrifying: a sneeze could make me pass out with the agony. A procession of doctors examined me and discussed what surgeries and treatments might work, but they couldn't be sure, of course. After an episode of chronic pain, lasting several weeks, I was finally scheduled to have major spinal surgery. I had been unable to stand for almost a week, and was being cared for by my now husband, who would help me into a room – generally the bathroom – before he left for work in the morning, then would help me back to bed on his return in the afternoon. I was barely more than existing.

Then, the day before the surgery, I stood up. It shouldn't perhaps have seemed like such a milestone, but it was to me. It was something that I had not been able to do the day before. I was excited. What if tomorrow I took a step? And then another? And so I cancelled the long-awaited surgery, and instead tried each day to accomplish something that I hadn't been able to do the day before.

Journey time was ridiculous – it could take me three minutes to cross a road, but I had such determination to get there that I just kept going. With a walking stick in one hand and a hot water bottle strapped to the base of my spine, I would force myself to shuffle oh so slowly to work, from my train carriage at London Bridge station to the Bank of England. One day, as I performed my odd and excruciating hobble across the bridge, I saw a woman running. She wore running shorts and a vest top, despite the chilly morning, and her toned legs carried her towards me in moments and past me in seconds. I wasn't prepared for the intense stab of jealousy I felt as I watched her.

Simply to be able to run felt like a pipe dream, but I wanted it so very much.

As I left work that evening, a security guard stood, arms folded, in the foyer of his building, watching the world go by. I could feel the warmth of his gaze take in the arduous progress of a sad-looking woman in the dusk outside. It was a fifteen-minute walk for most, but up to an hour for me. I paused for a moment, straightened up my back and took a few deep breaths. Gritting my teeth, I was mentally preparing myself for the next hundred metres when a car pulled up alongside me. The driver got out to open the passenger side door.

'I couldn't watch you any more,' the security guard told me. 'Come on, where are you going? I'll take you.'

I was glad it was dark inside his car, so he couldn't see me crying silently as he drove me to the entrance to the station. And in my head, tossed around with thoughts of love and gratitude for his compassion, was the clear promise to myself: *I will run again. I will run!*

The words of *Chicago Tribune* journalist Mary Schmich, made famous in the 1990s hit song 'Everybody's Free (To Wear Sunscreen)', ring very true:

> Enjoy your body, use it every way you can. Don't be afraid of it, or what other people think of it: it's the greatest instrument you'll ever own.[3]

Feeling true contentment and happiness, for me, invariably includes physical exercise. It reminds me that I have a healthy body, and that today, I am able to run or climb or swim. I can't predict tomorrow, but if today I can do these things, I am immeasurably grateful for that.

I have friends and colleagues for whom exercise was once something to be avoided at all costs. They are the 'after' story of the kids who were always picked last for the sports teams, and the ones tasked with handing out the bibs or keeping score rather than taking part. And they are the ones who finally realised, years later, that giving your own body the respect it deserves and keeping it fit and healthy is open to everyone. That taking a walk today and jog tomorrow feels amazing, and shedding kilos or building muscle and bursting through the finish line of your first race, high on endorphins, makes your heart want to burst (and of course makes your lungs feel that they already have!).

I've never met anyone who hasn't felt better, mentally and physically, for seeking out the exercise that works best for them and pursuing it, so I never tire of encouraging friends not to give up until they find their thing. In times of stress or challenge, you always have a trump card to play: the fall-back of physical exertion to flood your body with adrenaline and endorphins and remind yourself how alive and vital you are, and clear your mind of all thoughts other than the knowledge that you can!

> The miracle isn't that I finished. The miracle is that I had the courage to start.
> – John Bingham, *No Need for Speed: A Beginner's Guide to the Joy of Running*

Feeling emotionally secure, mentally balanced and physically fit are three of the pillars that hold the boundary of our comfort zone in place. Knowing where this boundary lies, and how and when to retreat behind it, is important. So too is recognising how and when we should step out beyond it.

WIDENING THE LIMITS

When fear is absent, so too are achievement and personal growth. Any goals worth pursuing have an intrinsic risk of failure, or they would be mere inevitabilities to be experienced along your chosen path. To feel that rush of pride and excitement once you've overcome your doubts and achieved what you'd feared you never would – that is only possible when you return the duvet to the bedroom, put your game face on and leap in with both feet. There is a time and a need for seeking refuge in your comfort zone. Failure, life's greatest teacher, is exhausting, and the strongest adventurer will need to take time out to catch her breath once in a while. But with each new adventure, you'll see that the boundaries of your comfort zone are drawn a little further out than they were before, and the fear that crept in at a certain point takes a little longer to arrive and lock its grip around you.

Understand what you need to make you feel safe, comfortable and in control. Go to that place when you need it. Heal there. But don't allow yourself to get too comfortable. There's a world to explore, and fears to overcome, so you mustn't allow yourself to linger too long. You will return, but you can expect it to look a little different when next you call in.

KEYS TO UNDERSTANDING YOUR COMFORT ZONE – AND WHEN TO LEAVE IT

- Understand what you need to feel good: do you need to run or rest? Socialise with friends or time for quiet reflection? Make a mental (or actual) note to prompt yourself to revel in the moment whenever you need to slow down, breathe deeply and feel good.

- Switch off external factors. Step away from your phone, your laptop and simply be in the moment. Whilst tech and screens are a great distraction, ask yourself whether being distracted is the way to bring you more happiness. Look at the scenery, don't take a photo of it. Talk, smile and laugh together, don't merely tweet alone.

- If you are a stranger to hard, physical exercise, brilliant! This is the equivalent of never having read *Harry Potter* or watched *Game of Thrones*: so much joy awaits you. It IS for you, and you DO deserve to have a body as fit and as strong as it can be. You just need to summon the energy to get started – and the resolve to stick with it.

- If you know that you're likely to take the path of least

resistance, set it up so that the path of least resistance is the one you actually want to take. Lay your gym kit out the night before. Drop your bike at the office so you have to cycle home on it. Arrange to meet with friends at the lake or pool, or even to meet online for words of mutual support and encouragement. Help yourself and each other out.

- Go to your comfort zone when you need it, then step boldly out of it to grow. Failing is not to be feared. In the words of performing artist and philanthropist Jayden Smith, 'Instead of saying "I failed today", let's challenge ourselves to say "I learned today. I grew today."'[4]

3. Get Your Brave On

That look on somebody's face when they've just done what they'd never imagined they could do. The teenagers pictured in the local paper collecting their exam results and glowing with relief and pride. The first successful descent of a piste on shaky skis. The goal scored against a team much stronger than your own. And the more dramatic examples: the mother who lifted up a car that had rolled forward onto her child.[1] The stranger who leaped onto the train tracks to rescue a toddler who had stepped forwards and fallen down.[2] On each occasion, did they know that they were brave enough or tenacious or instinctively swift enough to be able to do what they did?

The fear of failure or of not knowing the right answer can be paralysing. The fear that other people know better than you or can do it better than you, and will be silently (or worse, vocally) assessing and judging you and finding you lacking, is enough to derail many a great idea from ever getting off the starting blocks. But what if there is no binary, correct answer, but simply numerous shades of possible? And what if your approach or idea is as good as or better than many or any others?

Sometimes, we never truly know what we are capable of until we take the risk of trying.[3] There is a wealth of inspirational advice on this theme, possibly because it's such a key stumbling block for so many of us. In writing this book, I faltered initially, on the basis that if I did find a publisher who wanted to support me with it, I had the potentially more challenging issue of finding people (other than family and friends) who'd have any interest in reading it. I'd be lying if I said that the contemplation of both hurdles didn't stop me from writing for a while, and almost deterred me from doing so for good. The way forwards, for me, lay in realising one simple truth: the worst case scenario is entirely manageable.

THREE BUCKETFULS OF RISK

When assessing the risk to oneself in any situation, it generally falls into one of three buckets:

Bucket 1. The worst case scenario is entirely horrendous and potentially fatal —you should avoid like the plague

Correctly evaluating which option you're looking at is of course a significant part of the skill of risk assessment. It's easy to lump all unappealing or potentially terrifying possibilities into this first Bucket, but I'd suggest that it should in fact be the smallest receptacle into which great but misguided ideas are hurriedly tossed with a deep sigh of quiet relief. Getting blind drunk and driving home anyway because the journey is short, you know the way like the back of your hand, the road is mainly straight, you've driven it a million times, it's late and there aren't many people around… Just no. The risk that you'd pose to yourself and to others is unforgivably great. Yet this is less terrifying to many than the idea of giving a speech in public, or singing to a room full of people. Why are we sometimes so incapable of recognising where the real dangers in life are lurking?

Listen to your inner voice. And if your inner voice is absent or not to be trusted, test the idea out on somebody whose opinion you value. If they too are in short supply, try the trilogy of sustenance, exercise and sleep before making your mind up.

A former colleague always used to caution me against sending immediate replies to emails that I received late in the evening and which annoyed me to the point of sleeplessness. Instead, he suggested that I type my reply to get it off my chest but, before sending, take a walk (however brief: if I'm working from home, even a walk to the washing machine to shake out and hang up some clothes is enough if there's no time for a walk with the dog or a run), have something to eat or drink (hunger and thirst can really affect your mood, so check that you're not getting hungry and ratty, or dehydrated and therefore irritable), and then, importantly, sleep. When Bagheera told Mowgli in *The Jungle Book* that 'things will look better in the morning', the insightful black panther knew exactly what he was talking about. And when you need to make important decisions, such as 'Is this in fact a Bucket 1 scenario?', you need to be on your A game.

Sleep on it

The benefit of sleep is something about which I frequently wax lyrical. And I am an expert on this point, not because of my excellent discipline and fastidious adherence to a healthy sleep pattern. I wish that were the case. But no: I have regularly made poor decisions about whether simply drawing a line under the day and going to bed, so that I can pick up where I've left off feeling refreshed and focused in the morning after a night of good quality sleep, would be more beneficial than plugging away late into the night at whatever I'm doing.

Things seem worse late at night, or whenever you're at your most tired. When you've worked all day in the home, out of the home, physically or mentally – it all adds up to the same thing: when you are exhausted, your decision making becomes lousy. The answer: Go. To. Bed.

Bucket 2. The worst case scenario is not quite as apocalyptic as it might seem – you will survive. You should go for it

For example, taking a new and terrifyingly challenging job with colleagues who you've yet to meet and who might not get your sense of humour and with tasks that might be beyond you... A very clear Bucket 2. You might learn from the experience and flourish, steadily going on to greater things as you win your colleagues over with your personality, hard work and great leadership. Even in the unlikely event that all of the Doomsday scenarios materialise, you will survive. Not being the smartest person in the office isn't fatal, and neither is losing out on first place in the popularity contest. Realising the job is simply not for you after all, and then setting off for pastures new – all these things may be temporarily destabilising, but a resilient person will bounce back.

Climb to victory, one step at a time

I was watching my niece in the playground recently. Climbing up the steps to the baby slide, manoeuvring her chunky little thighs past the handrail and down onto the cold steel of the slide occupied her fully for about five minutes. Soon enough, it was clear that the thrill had worn off. She had clocked her big sister whizzing down the bigger slide, and suddenly the excitement of the baby slide had fizzled out.

The challenge of the bigger slide, though, was more than a little intimidating. She stood next to the steps, eyeing up the metal rungs that disappeared far above her messy blonde head, and watched her sister racing up and whizzing down. With a brave little sigh, she set off to have a go for herself. These steps had bigger spaces between each one, and she could only make it from one to the next with a lot of effort and whole-body clambering, step, by step, by step. The bigger children were climbing over her, missing the two steps that she occupied at any given point in the process, swinging up and past to the top of the slide, again and again. It didn't deter her at all. Finally, she got there.

She looked incredulous and delighted as I smiled and waved and cheered, and she did a few excited jumps on the top steps in obvious celebration of her achievement. She didn't slide down immediately, not because she was afraid of the descent, but because she was so clearly relishing the sense of victory as she stood at the top of the mountain she had conquered. Finally, she took her spot on the slide and, grinning broadly, whizzed down. After a celebratory hug and a request for clapping (which I readily fulfilled), she was off up again: less effort this time. She knew that she had this.

Then, she spotted her older cousins, as they climbed up the *biggest* slide...

How often do we take the approach demonstrated by my little niece?

How often do we assess the challenges ahead, feel intimidated by them, but take them on headfirst anyway, and then truly celebrate when we nail it? Possibly not often enough. I've heard it explained away as a British thing or as a woman thing – to shy away from applause for fear of looking boastful. Perhaps it's both. Perhaps it's neither. Perhaps it's simply a human thing: if we don't try, we cannot fail; and if we don't announce our successes, nobody will point out that it's all been a misunderstanding, and our win isn't the win that we originally believed it to be.

There is an alternative. We can see the challenge, recognise it, understand it, appreciate that there's a real possibility that we might fail, but then do it anyway. If we have a go, there's a possibility we will fail. If we let fear of failure prevent us from even attempting it, we can be certain that we cannot succeed.

It is human nature to flick to fight-or-flight mode when faced with a serious challenge: the reaction is not simply mental. Our heart races; our skin gets clammy. When I'm feeling particularly stressed, my vision blurs and I feel physically sick. But the threat might not be a realistic one. The word 'fear' can be broken down into the acronym 'False Expectations Appearing Real'. We can be truly brilliant at painting an utterly believable vision of impending doom for ourselves, when in fact, the fear of what may happen is by no means about the probable, or often even the possible. So why do we do it? It's simple self-preservation: if we don't take any risks, we can't hurt or embarrass ourselves. So our subconscious creates these compelling stories to prevent us from daring to try. Fortunately though, our subconscious is not operating alone. We can spur our conscious mind into action, to talk sense (or perhaps talk bravery) to ourselves and, provided this is truly a Bucket 2 situation, focus instead on a positive rhetoric to help us face the situation that we fear head-on.

Sometimes I play 'follow the disaster': if the result that I fear happens, what then? Let's take the fear of delivering a speech on stage: everybody will be staring at me (excellent! You'll have their attention), judging me (great – truly concentrating on what you're saying and processing it. You're having an impact), and I might stumble over my words or forget what I need to say (in neither case will the world end, nor is any dire consequence likely to follow). But what if my speech is hopeless, I lose the respect of the audience, it harms my reputation at work, I lose my job, I can't pay the mortgage, I move to a smaller house and look for a new role...? However I've played it, I've never ended up with... *and then my family and I all suffer catastrophic harm and die.*

Making mistakes is the most important way to learn, so taking a path so risk averse that you lose all the possibilities of making mistakes means bypassing too many opportunities that might bring joy and a true sense of accomplishment. In any event, the mistakes are often the most enjoyable parts! As the American writer and artist Suzy Kassem puts it: 'Doubt kills more dreams than failure ever will.'

Bucket 3. The worst case scenario is entirely horrendous and poten-
tially fatal, but you have no alternative option – you should summon
your courage, and do it afraid

The third and final bucket is in many ways my favourite: The
experiences that are collected here will leave you with that air-
punching feeling of immense pride, incredulity and holy-crap-
I-did-it-osity.

On my meandering trip around Latin America in 2001, my
friends and I found ourselves in a bus station in Belize with a
couple of hours to kill. John decided to take a rest under a tree
in the sun, enjoying a chance to sit and relax after being jolted
around on a bus for every minute of the last twelve hours since
leaving Guatemala. Fannie and I, however, decided to take a
walk. We were right on the coast, in a beautiful country that
we would soon be leaving, so every chance to enjoy more of
it before we left would be a bonus. We crossed the road away
from the bus station and walked down to the shore. It wasn't
exactly as we'd hoped. The stretch where we'd entered was
strewn with sad mounds of plastic bottles, cans and discarded
building materials. Meshed wire fences slashed the shoreline
into boxed off sections. Standing on a short wooden jetty, a little boy tossed stones at the water. He turned and watched us
as we walked across to him. His name was Jesus (yes, it is at
this point in the story that my friends generally begin to doubt
the accuracy of the tale, but truly…), and he suggested that
we walk south along the shore, as the beach there was much
cleaner and more pleasant.

And Jesus was right: past the first fence and then the second,
the scene began to look more like the ones in the brochures,
and less like the ones in the ocean wildlife charity campaign
posters. Deep in conversation, we planned the next few days of

our trip, and recounted the highlights of the last few weeks of travel.

It was Fannie who noticed them first. She stopped and stood completely still, staring wide eyed up the beach ahead of us, where a beautiful white house stood partly hidden behind a screen of amaryllis and honeysuckle. It was by far the most impressive building we'd seen since arriving in the town and, I suddenly realised, it was being ably protected against unwanted visitors by four colossal and muscular Doberman dogs. My admiration of the house and the animals was dwarfed, however, by my deep concern that they were, at that moment, hurtling towards us as swiftly as their legs could carry them. It was truly like a scene from a film: the furious barking with spittle swinging from rows of gnashing teeth; the clouds of sand kicked up by sixteen large, pounding paws as the stretch of land between them and us rapidly disappeared. And the thought process, spooling through options and possibilities: the initial naïve belief that nothing too bad is likely to happen. Getting mauled by a pack of guard dogs is the sort of thing you read about in the newspapers happening to Someone Else, as you give a shake of the head and a sad tut that such a thing has happened to poor clueless holiday makers. Then you turn the page and carry on with life.

Yet here we were, and here they were – standing still and hoping that this was a Bucket 2 occasion did not seem like a viable position to maintain. Grabbing Fannie's hand and dragging her with me, I ran to the sea. There was no possibility that we would outrun the dogs – that much was clear – but there was a chance that we might be able to outswim them. We kicked our way through the murky surf until we were chest deep, then swam, and swam and swam. We kept heading out further to sea, Fannie screaming at me between salty gasps, 'Sarah! We are about to die! Why the f*** are you laughing?!'

But it had suddenly become obvious: this was a Bucket 3 occasion! The worst case scenario was entirely horrendous and potentially fatal, but we had no alternative option: we simply had to summon our courage, and do it afraid (and slightly hysterical). After some minutes of standing knee deep in the water and warning us off their shore, the dogs threw a few more desultory growls our way, then retreated to the house, their mission accomplished.

Fannie and I turned and swam back down the coast to where we'd first found Jesus. Again, the boy silently watched our approach, possibly noticing that we looked altogether more exhausted than when we'd first met. Arms aching, Fannie and I heaved ourselves out of the water and lay breathing heavily on the jetty at Jesus's feet. For a few moments, the only sound was the gentle lapping of the waves against the shore, and the deep gasps of Fannie and me as we recovered our breath.

'Why would you want to swim in there?' Jesus asked, curious but dispassionate. 'It's quite dangerous, as the piranhas come in to feed at the sewage outlet.' And he pointed towards the area of water from which we'd just emerged. Sure enough, it was thick and cloudy and uninviting.

'You didn't mention the piranhas!' Fannie growled through gritted teeth. She pointed out that the scenic stroll he'd sent us on happened to pass by the apparently private property of several fierce dogs.

'Oh, I'm sure they were just playing,' I lied. 'They'd probably never have bitten us.'

Jesus looked at me incredulously. 'Oh no!' he corrected. 'They're my aunt's guard dogs, perhaps I should have said. They're trained to kill.'

A cold hose down by a bemused petrol station attendant later, and with the smell of salty sewage beginning to fade, Fannie and I made our way back to John and the next leg of our bus journey. I reflected on how well spent our time had been: when faced with a pack of angry and bloodthirsty hounds trying to kill me, and an uncertain escape through piranha-infested sewage, in a life and death situation where every option was terrifying, I now knew that I could choose the least horrendous option, and survive it. (I also learned that it can be difficult to correctly assess which Bucket you're looking at, but triumph can be found through any of them.)

Needless to say, the third Bucket also captures unavoidably tragic situations, such as terminal illness and serious injury. The rule is the same, though: if an experience has to be endured, your only choice might be your own state of mind whilst you endure it. And it is a choice, so choose bold; choose hopeful; choose fearless. Fear is only helpful if it drives you to take some positive action as a result. If no positive action is possible, try choosing *not* to be afraid: pretend to be someone brave and, after a little practice, you mightn't need to pretend so much after all. As Christopher Robin tells Winnie-the-Pooh: 'You are braver than you believe, stronger than you seem, and smarter than you think.'[4]

KEYS TO GETTING YOUR BRAVE ON

- **Risk is good: do not be afraid of risk. Instead, acknowledge it, mitigate it and plan for it. Do not simply avoid it entirely, or you will also be avoiding opportunities to develop and progress in life.**

- **Set yourself up well to make good decisions, particularly where it really matters: eat, exercise and sleep before making a decision if you doubt your objectivity, and get a second opinion from somebody you trust if you're still in doubt.**

- Think through the worst case scenarios and objectively assess how likely they are to materialise. If the benefit of doing it is valuable, and you're likely to survive it, do it! If you want to do it but you can't conquer your fear, you'll just have to do it afraid.

- If you can do something to improve the result, do it. If nothing you can do will make any difference to the outcome, you can still determine your own mind-set. Worrying in such situations is entirely pointless.

- Never hold back from stating the obvious. What is as clear as day to one person as a result of the lessons they've learned on their journey might never have occurred to another. Let it not be you who fails to mention the piranhas!

- Making mistakes is the most important way to learn. Treat each one as a triumph: another lesson successfully learned. In the words of the inventor Thomas A. Edison: 'I have not failed. I've just found 10,000 ways that won't work.'

Part II
Come What May...

None of us knows quite what might be lurking around the corner for us. The fantastic promotion and the move to a beautiful new home, or the tragic death of someone we love, and a period of uncertainty for ourselves. Being able to predict accurately what lies ahead is as unnecessary as it is impossible: as humans, we learn through challenge, and we become stronger every time we realise what we have achieved as a result of something we never saw coming or never imagined that we could overcome. Taking away the surprise element would, in part, be taking away the opportunity to grow.

Our inability to prophesise should not, however, detract from our ability to prepare. If I were being taken on a surprise holiday, I might not know where I was headed, but I'd still pack a passport, a bikini, an evening outfit and a few daytime options, just in case. So what does this mean for life generally? How can we plan for everything, just in case...? The key, as this part will explore, is to ensure that you are as strong and as anchored as possible, with the right network in place to lean in and lend support if you need it. And keep your eyes open: be aware of how the landscape might be developing and shifting around you, so that you are familiar with it, and ready and able to respond positively, come what may…

4. Find A Role You Love

Sitting in the warm, dim lecture theatre before day one in my new job as a trainee lawyer, surrounded by eager minds and gently sweating bodies, I battled somnolence as speaker after speaker took to the stage, and informed, inspired and implored. Ours were the great legal minds of the future. We would work tirelessly – through the night, and into the next day (and perhaps the next) – in order to serve our clients in the manner expected of a lawyer at a Magic Circle law firm...[1]

I was unconvinced. I had no doubt that I'd give it my best shot. But if I was struggling to stay awake even after a good night's rest at my mum's house, how, in this new world, after spending up to forty-eight hours in my new Reiss suit and slightly pinchy shoes trotting along the carpeted corridors of The Firm, would I ever be able to stay conscious, let alone spout legal excellence? These were surely no more than scare tactics, intended to send the weak back to the Home Counties as soon as the coffee break with mini croissants was over. I would not be deterred.

With the sixty new legal trainees gathered together, a fashion advisor took to the stage. Whilst our university and law school tutors had helped to shape our academic credentials, the question of whether our dress sense was apposite to our burgeoning careers in the law had thus far fallen to chance. This would not do. There were a number of common wardrobe mistakes and pitfalls that could easily be avoided with the help of a printed sheet and a little audience participation. A double-breasted jacket on a young man not yet into his heart attack years: no. A skirt too short and heels too flat. Oh no no no. Jewellery and make up: just enough, and never none. Stubble: an emphatic no. In our pairs, we stood and assessed each other, closely, constructively, brutally. *According to the sheet, your suit is a little tight. And the trousers: perhaps slightly too short? Thank you. And you look super, but perhaps a touch of make up tomorrow? Yes, you are absolutely right. Thank you.* And then we sat down again. We were ready to step forwards as the new generation of lawyers made in London.

As the sheen slowly wore off our new kitten heels and our career choices, what remained was a deepening understanding of what it meant to work. I don't say this in a disparaging way: the opportunity to learn and develop was second to none, and there's no doubt that we were well looked after: seminars on the thornier areas of law with which we needed to grapple; beautiful surroundings with super bright colleagues (both adjectives interchangeable) and a clean shirt and toothbrush available for those occasions when days merged. Yet a recent graduate's idea of the realities of a demanding and well-paid career are perhaps more focused on the perks, the suits and the after-work cocktails that could now be afforded even outside of the Student Union happy hour. All of those visions materialised, but so too did the feeling of utter exhaustion.

I paced Fleet Street at 11pm one Friday night, trying to hail a cab, surrounded by lolling, singing, drunken mobs, revelling in the start of their weekend. Sober and broken, I just wanted to get home for the first time since Wednesday. Occupying a position both as the absolute elite (so we were reminded) and, simultaneously, the plankton echelon within the firm, was mentally and physically draining. Was this what I had studied for, for all these years? It was. Did it soothe my soul and make me excited on a Sunday night, eager for the week ahead to begin? It certainly did not.

For seven years, I commuted into the city and poured every ounce of energy into developing as a lawyer. At one firm, and then a second, with a higher salary and longer hours, I learned from incredible practitioners what to aim for, and what never ever to do.

In one meeting in a city hotel conference room, an African oil tycoon insidiously taunted the Jewish lawyer who was representing his counterparty with repeated anti-Semitic jibes and comments *sotto voce*. Despite several clear warnings from my boss, Jennifer, that such comments were unacceptable to everybody present, the tycoon persisted. Pushed too far, the Jewish lawyer launched himself across the table and towards the throat of the man insulting him. In the fracas that followed, as the gentlemen and the sandwiches were hurriedly cleared from the table top, the fear that the entire negotiation, which had cost all parties dear in many respects, might fail as a result was palpable.

Cutting through the fray, Jennifer firmly and clearly set out the basis upon which we would continue, eliciting the agreement from all in the room, as to what was, and what was not going to be tolerated going forward. Then, taking her chair, she returned to the last point discussed, and continued as though nothing at all had just happened. Her refusal to accept the inexcusable, and her calm in the face of madness, stayed with me and inspired me.

When I was heavily pregnant with my first daughter, but

with no time to slow the pace and take life a little easier, my working week regularly exceeded 100 hours. Of course it sounds like insanity now, but, at the time, there was too much pressure just to keep working to be able to step back and ask myself what the heck I was thinking, and why I didn't simply return to my bed and stay there. It was normal, and was accepted by everyone around me that this was simply how life was. And it wasn't all bad: the friendships forged in the office at 3am, when the only sources of energy and refreshment were ice cream stowed earlier in the office freezer, emergency Creme Eggs, and reviving cucumber and mint facial wipes, can last a lifetime. And the strength taken from a discreet smile and a whispered urge of *illegitimi non carborundum* (a mock-Latin aphorism meaning 'don't let the bastards grind you down') by the revered arbitrator of a multi-billion dollar dispute, after a day with more hectoring from my own boss than from the opponent side in the arbitration, still boosts my courage today.

The last few weeks before my maternity leave passed and, as I walked out through the colossal polished glass doors with my potted peace lily tucked under my arm, I was in no doubt at all that I would not be working there again. There's not a moment of my life there that I regret and, given the chance to change any of it, I would leave every minute exactly as it was. But, for my future, at that moment I chose something different.

Any challenging situation can be endured provided there is (i) some benefit to you in enduring it, and (ii) a goal or an endpoint, for either the challenging element or the endurance itself to cease. This chapter considers how best to extract as much benefit as possible from any situation, and how to assess whether the time has come to make a change, and what that change should be.

Sarah Nelson Smith

EXPERIENCE

Experience: that most brutal of teachers. But you learn, my God,
do you learn.
  – C. S. Lewis (attrib.)

Work. As soon as you realise that you want something or that
you may want something that money can buy, work. As soon
as you feel that boredom and complacency might creep into
your life and start to sour your appreciation of your fortunes,
whether many or few, work. As soon as you find yourself
judging people or struggling to empathise with their position,
work, until you have taken the roles at each point of the career
ladder, and familiarised yourself with the highs and lows that
each position brings with it. No doubt you'll still judge – having worked in the food industry and restaurants, poor service
and process drives me crazy, while my husband pretty much
takes whatever is served up to him; but now I'm able to give
considered, rational feedback based on an understanding of
what *should* reasonably be happening.

I was eleven when I got my first job. It seems incredible now
(indeed, it seemed incredible then), but a local family asked me
to babysit for them. Living in a small Surrey village, my world
was fully accessible by bicycle, so I arrived at the agreed time,
ready to watch the baby as he slept. At home, my mother sat
anxiously by the telephone, having instructed me to call her if
the baby woke, cried, rolled over, and also if he didn't wake,
didn't cry or didn't roll over. I'd managed to resist taking the
hand mirror that she tried to slip into my rucksack ('Hold it just
under his nose as he sleeps: if it mists up, you'll know that he's
breathing') and off I went. I had homework in my bag and a
book to read. I was ready to babysit.

The mother opened the door, a wriggling infant in her arms.
'He's due a feed,' she explained, 'but we're running late, so are

you okay to feed him?' I nodded, slack jawed as I followed her into the nursery, where she picked out a pale blue brushed cotton babygro. 'Just pop him into this afterwards, and he'll be ready to sleep by about 8pm.' The mirror was not needed: the hungry guzzling as he made light work of a bottle of milk, and the hilarious air-boxing and kicking as I lay him on a towel on the carpet to get him changed and ready for bed left me no time to check his vital signs.

The sense of responsibility I felt towards that little boy was almost overwhelming. Until that point, I had only ever thought of myself as a child, to be looked after and cared for and protected from harm by others. Now, one Saturday evening, that role had been reversed, and I was responsible for the wellbeing of a tiny human. When he was fed, burped, cleaned up and tucked in, I sat watching him sleep with a sense of amazement. He was beautiful and incredible, and had been entrusted to me. I had been *trusted* to do something of which I hadn't even realised I was capable. And this was only the start.

The feeling of being trusted to fulfil a useful role was heady and addictive, and the fact that, in each role, my work was worthy of payment was a new and wonderfully empowering feeling. I wanted horse riding lessons. As the Bank of Mum and Dad had declined the request, I worked every hour of my summer holidays, mucking out, cleaning leathers and grooming horses, in return for thirty precious minutes on horseback each week being instructed on how to ride. Certainly, my negotiating abilities then were poor, and an observer might comment that the deal I struck was a pretty rubbish one from my position, but for a girl wanting to spend time with horses to understand them better, and learn how to care for them properly, every hour of the week was valuable tuition. Sitting atop the haystack in the cool of the barn, eating my sandwiches with the other yard hands and the newest batch of feral kittens for company, I felt pretty good about life.

And so it continued: pot washer and sandwich maker in the golf club kitchen, checkout assistant in Sainsbury's, babysitter to the majority of the village, cinema usher at the university arts centre, barmaid in a smoky and packed Irish pub, holiday rep in Northern Greece, English teacher in Southern China... In each role, the stories and the experiences exceeded the pay by miles, making me infinitely richer as a result.

CREATE YOUR OWN PATCHWORK OF EXPERIENCES

Nothing will work unless you do.
– Maya Angelou

Try everything. A patchwork quilt of experiences, whether in employment or otherwise, gives you the opportunity through trial and error to get to know and understand what's really right for you. This is an easy piece of advice to follow as a six-teen-year-old looking for any sort of job that will take you and pay minimum wage, but perhaps more challenging as a middle-aged parent with a mortgage. Yet it's perhaps all the more important to reassess and to force yourself to question what you like and what you're looking for, when you're at risk of settling for something that you don't, and you weren't.

FLYING IN A NEW DIRECTION

Aged fifty-three, my Auntie Nikki, who had built her career in education, acknowledged that the changing demands of her job were slowly eroding the pleasure that she had derived from it for many years. The sinking, back-to-work-tomorrow Sunday evening feeling began on Friday, with the knowledge that two short days of weekend would pass all too swiftly and, like Groundhog Day, it would all begin again.

She began fantasising about an escape. She would be a bus driver! She would drive the 289 to Elmers End each day, and see little old ladies on and off the bus with a helping hand and a cheery wave. There would be no stress at all, just a big red bus and the open (albeit very congested south London) roads.

This, my cousin told her, was a bad idea. He was working for British Airways at the time and enthusiastically told his mum all about his adventures as ground crew and then as cabin crew with the airline. He told her about some of the other people on his training course: two ex-teachers training for a new career in aviation at the age of fifty-something. And the idea took hold. It seemed entirely impractical, though, what with her full-time job and mortgage to pay, and not being in the main demographic for air hostesses. The sensible, easy option would have been to delicately pack up the dream and pop it in the attic together with the other hopes that fell by the wayside over the years. So she applied.

Explaining to her employer that she would be taking some unpaid leave, Auntie Nikki began her six-week training as cabin crew with First Choice. Most of her new colleagues were the same age as her son, yet it was entirely immaterial: wearing her shocking pink jacket, skirt and scarf, she was just another member of the flight crew. And she loved it! Her working day began as she arrived at the airport, and ended as she walked out of it: she took nothing home with her, other than photographs and mementoes from the many places she visited that she would never otherwise have had the opportunity to see, and memories of wonderful times spent enjoying a completely different life with a completely different group of new friends. The burden of life as she knew it lifted.

Just as she'd planned, she stayed in the job for six months.

Her previous employer understood her need to try something new, and held her position open for her to return to once she'd turned in her jacket and name badge, and closed that fun, but temporary, new chapter. On her return to teaching, she took the chance to negotiate a new role, with greater focus on the elements that she found most rewarding, and leaving behind the parts that she didn't.

So what was the point of such a huge but brief career change, for only six months? Because (and apologies for the cliché) we have only one brief but wonderful life, so it's our obligation to make it as rich as possible while we can. And because what might seem impossible rarely is. Auntie Nikki told me: 'In my uniform, I looked like a colossal great marshmallow, but still, it was the best thing I ever did.'

What wonderful, impossible thing would you do, what change would you make if you didn't let the initial questions about practicalities kill the dream before it ever had a chance to take hold? Have you ever listened to the neighbour or colleague talking excitedly about their imminent move overseas, and thought, a little jealously, that it simply wouldn't be possible for you because… And have you, some months later, looked at their sunny Instagram posts with a pang? Might it be that it was utterly impractical and almost completely impossible for them too, before they figured out how to make it a reality? Dust down the dreams that you shelved some time ago, and look at them again, through a more adventurous, more imaginative lens.

UNDERSTAND WHAT YOU'RE LOOKING FOR

I have lost count of the number of times that I have ducked into the supermarket for milk and a newspaper, only to emerge an hour or so later, struggling under the weight of the irresistible fresh fruit and bread, three jars of pesto, an equal number of tubes of toothpaste on special offer and all the numerous other excellent but arguably non-essential and surplus-to-requirements items. And frequently without either the milk or newspaper that I went in for in the first place.

What went wrong? I was wooed by the strategically placed temptations, and my focus shifted from what I knew I needed to how I could potentially make use of something else entirely. Certainly the items I purchased served a purpose and were appreciated as and when they came to be consumed. But there was still that pang of disappointment when, later that afternoon, I wanted to sit down with a cappuccino and the newspaper, and had to settle instead for mint tea and the news online. In the context of a Sunday afternoon, this scenario is mildly irritating. In the context of a potentially life-changing career move or first step onto the career ladder, it has scope to be significantly worse.

There are many things that the brave and the bold will leave to chance, letting karma or fortune or serendipity call the shots. Your career should not be one such thing. Take the time to think through what you really want, what you need, and what your motivations are for looking to take or avoid taking this step this time.

WHAT'S KEEPING YOU FROM THE JOB OF YOUR DREAMS?

So many of us do what we do because it's what we've always done. We spend so long training or qualifying for a particular job or profession that it would 'be a waste' not to use the qualifications that we have. Or we have chosen to live in a certain area in order to be close to our job or business (or found a job or established a business so as to be convenient for home), and switching either would bring unnecessary disruption. This is not quite as logical as it initially sounds. If a person has nothing, none of your experience, skills or current employment, what they *do* have is the freedom to go anywhere, and set up in anything that they choose to do (and if this is you – if you have nothing but this book and a plan to seek new employment, the world truly is your oyster, and I hope you cast your net as wide as possible in considering all of the myriad options that are open to you, and which might bring you joy and fulfilment). Why then should a person have less freedom and opportunity simply because they have already started their journey down a particular path?

> Each decision we make must be right for the moment that we make it. And no decision should be treated as final: you should regularly revisit it. What you are, is what you have been. What you'll be is what you do now.
> – Buddha

When weighing up your next move, there are a number of elements you might want to take into account:

Financial considerations: the base salary or potential income is clearly one factor in the decision to be made, but it is only one of many. Weigh up the impact of any other perks, from car allowance, family health insurance, bonus (and factor in the likelihood of such bonus actually being paid whether in part or in full, given that most are discretionary), pension contributions, cost of travel, and additional associated costs and benefits. If you only have twenty days' holiday per year, but have the option to buy more to make it up to the twenty-five or thirty days if you really want, what's the impact on the remainder of the package? And are there other perks that you'd want to take advantage of? Childcare vouchers, season ticket loan, the option to buy a bicycle from pre-taxed income, other discounts – all these add up and may make a seemingly average proposition much more appealing. Is there the option of taking share options or equity in the company? Depending on the company, this might be an excellent top-up or a complete punt – gold dust or sawdust.

For the self-employed, there are other ways of benefitting from perks previously only available to employees. Joining communities such as WeWork gives access to more than simply office space: the leverage of the global membership network is used to negotiate discounted services and products, and creates a circle of entrepreneurial self-starters.

Geography: living next door to the office is as hellish an idea for some as a two-hour commute seems for others. One of my closest friends has a forty-minute cycle to work along a pretty, well-lit canal. This seemed both perfect and incredibly fortunate to me, until she corrected me. Yes, it seemed perfect to her too, but not fortunate so much as well planned: after a lot of trial and error, she had finally found a part of the world that she knew she wanted to live in. So she rented a flat there, managing a hideous and exhausting commute, until she finally found the job she wanted in the area she loved, and could make plans to buy a home. She could then, finally, exchange the hours spent each day on a bus for the scenic cycle ride that I envied. There were areas in which she was prepared to compromise – such as renting for a while until the other pieces fell into place – and others that were non-negotiable.

A train commute has the benefit of creating time to read, listen to music, work or simply be. Yet it also comes with the challenge of cancelled trains, the wrong sort of leaves / snow / fellow commuters, and no guarantee of a seat. Driving to work gives you time to make phone calls (safely on hands free), listen to music, or simply decompress and prepare for the transition from hectic work life to high octane family madness, with the benefit of a guaranteed seat every time. For me, the M25 car park had its challenges, however, and driving from door to door meant that, on a particularly busy day, I could find myself climbing into bed in the evening without having spent any time at all outdoors. Now, I cycle a 50-mile round trip to London a few days a week, or take the train when I want a rest. I love the exercise, the me-time, and the sporadic companionship of the hordes of cyclists who throng into the city together as my journey nears its end. I hate punctures with a passion though, and an evening out takes a little forethinking of the plan to get home.

There is simply no correct answer, but rather a range of possibilities that you can squeeze the best out of, or rule out entirely. Think it through carefully, and realistically.

Personal development and growth: this concept means everything to some people, and is no more than a string of irritating buzz words to others. For either type of individual to get it wrong, and to accept a role in an organisation where the culture and attitude towards personal development are not aligned with their own, lies somewhere between bold and foolish. Of course, a hardy flower can grow and flourish in a barren landscape, but it would do so more easily in a fertile spot, with the nutrients that it needs to survive. So too is it possible to push yourself relentlessly to pursue the path of self-improvement, but finding others to help you on the journey is tough when they think it's all a load of nonsense and you should just get your head down and get back to work.

With your own business, the opportunities to grow may well be limitless. Do you have the discipline and rigour to plan out what you want to achieve, both for yourself, and for your team or employees? And to then hold yourself accountable for achieving it, seeking the help you might need along the way in order to do so?

Spend time truly understanding what you'd be getting yourself into, and be realistic about the impact that you will be able to have on the job, and that the job will have on you.

Stepping stone to something better / different: if you are in a role that you know is not sustainable, or which is wrong for you in some way (whether making you miserable, or paying you a pittance), is there a good enough reason for you to stay in it? Most people can put up with hardship if there's an end in sight. The pain of childbirth seemed much easier to handle to me than the excruciating pain in my spine that I'd suffered for years. It might be that the latter was simply more intense. Or it could be that I knew that the pain of childbirth would pass (no doctor ever simply left the baby in utero, deeming the challenge of exit too overwhelming to entertain). Back pain, however, can last a lifetime, and without hope and confidence that it will pass, the pain can seem unbearable. In a work context, if you simply want to get the experience or qualification that a certain role will offer, or the bonus that will pay out after a certain period, there's a lot of imperfection that can be borne in that time. And having a realistic expectation of how much (or how little) you'll enjoy the role in the meantime means that the bar is potentially set low enough for you to be able to surpass and pleasantly surprise yourself!

More or less challenge: some of the organisations I've worked in have an 'up or out' policy; one must keep developing and growing and rising through the ranks, or else pack one's bags and prepare for the org announcement: '*It is with mixed emotions that we must inform you that Jim has decided to leave to pursue other opportunities…*' Would this suit you? Are you looking for the chance to progress and for your salary and job title to do likewise, or do you long for a role where you can work each day, safe in the knowledge that you know exactly what you're doing, and you can simply get on and do it without any pressure to change? The slight caution I'd give about the latter position is that, to a certain extent, change is inevitable.

My window cleaner, for example, has changed his business by creating a great website with functions enabling potential customers to check on a map whether they fall within his area, use a calculator tool to check the approximate cost that his service would be in relation to their home, and for existing customers to check and settle their bill online. He's also focused on site-optimisation to ensure that he's appearing in the online searches for 'find a window cleaner near me' that he'd like to pop up in. The point is that ten years ago he'd have simply dropped a card through the letterbox of households in his area, then turned up with a bucket when called to do so. He didn't have to change, but by doing so, he has kept ahead of the competition and won more customers than he might have been able to do otherwise. Standing still can mean falling behind or falling out of the game altogether. Be prepared to embrace change.

Culture: when organisations talk about the great culture that they foster, this almost seems like a cliché now. What does it actually mean? I visited one organisation and afterwards gushed to my friend Clare on WhatsApp:

> *It's fantastic! Been chatting with the lovely receptionist, invited to a party, met a lady in the loos who offered me some of her perfume after I said I liked it, and am now sitting with a glass of prosecco that someone gave me. This place is great!*

My rational friend replied:

> *This is all very lovely but they do not address the things that annoy you in your current role, ergo, do not constitute reasons to join. Keep it real. Glad of prosecco and a spritz of perfume... you are a cheap hire!*

Look through the perfume spritz and the free prosecco, to the things that will really make a difference. What's the vision of the company? What are the shared values and attitudes of the people within it? Is it each person for themselves in an effort to meet personal targets, or is reward achieved through team goals and other less tangible factors? Is there a clear hierarchy that must be observed if you are to succeed there, or does a meritocracy provide the framework for progression? None is right or wrong, but it would be wise to understand what you'd be getting yourself into before you get yourself into it.

Quality of life: this means whatever you want it to mean. For me, I want to work hard, and I know that long and unsociable hours spent at a keyboard are built into my psyche. However, friends, family and exercise are also important to me: I'll never miss my daughters' sports days or school concerts, and I need to have an opportunity to weave exercise into my weekly regime. I check and reply to work emails on holiday, albeit in pockets of the day and night when my family don't notice. When working from home, I make my phone calls whilst walking the dog, and when in the office, I hold meetings with colleagues while walking a circuit down to the river, over the bridge and back to the office as we talk. I also travel on weekends when I need to, take and make work calls at any time of the day or night, and am prepared to drop everything and jump right in when my colleagues or company need me. It wouldn't suit everybody, but this, to me, is a good quality of life. Certainty or flexibility? Familiar routine or unknown challenges from day to day? What does it mean for you?

There is absolutely no right or wrong answer in choosing what is right for you at any particular time. Many of us are, however, guilty of ruling out possibilities simply because they are different from what we are used to, or because we can't immediately picture how it might work. Start from the presumption that anything is possible, and work backwards to figure out how. Friends with very different viewpoints and a couple of hours to spare (and perhaps a decent bottle of wine or several) can help a great deal with this process.

KEYS TO FINDING THE RIGHT ROLE FOR YOU, FOR NOW

- Meet people who do the role you'd like to do: understand why they do it and what they perceive to be the great and not-so-great aspects of it. Don't be afraid to ask for guidance and advice: it's an honour to be asked, and people are often very happy to help if you only let them know that you need it.

- Take on a variety of roles and experiences: each one pays the bills, or presents an opportunity to learn something new about the job, the people who work there, and yourself. Seize such opportunities.

- Have the courage to invite challenge into your life through change, rather than always accepting the status quo. This is not about compromising your values: it's simply being practical and realistic. However...

- ... be wary of assuming that the grass is always greener elsewhere, and that you need to disrupt in order to progress. Have you truly exhausted all avenues to learn, develop and grow where you are? A track record of job-hopping on a CV might concern potential employers, and may need to be explained.

- The right thing for right now might be the wrong thing for the next phase of your life. Check yourself every so often to make sure that you're doing what's right for you and your family.

- Make sure you know what you're looking for before you set off to find it. Don't be dazzled by the free prosecco if you'd be compromising on more material factors to get it.

5. Find Your Tribe

In 1666, a young Sir Isaac Newton was relaxing under an apple tree when an apple fell on his head. A seminal moment for science and the advancement of human understanding, as it inspired his theory of gravity. Many years later, in Selsdon public library in 1993, I sat at a large cluster of tables poring over illicit copies of *Jackie* magazine, learning much about how to have perfect party hair, what 'dreamboy' Jason Donovan looks for in a girl, and how to tell if a guy is into you (as a robust fourteen-year-old girl who had yet to master the art of perfect party hair, I had to admit he invariably wasn't), when I stumbled across a new theory that would forever change my outlook on life. An insightful article on spring-cleaning one's wardrobe. It acknowledged the difficulty encountered by many in throwing out a beloved t-shirt that has been worn to death one summer and is now only good for using as a duster. And it gave a sage nod to the guilt one might feel in having a wonderful and expensive article of clothing that might be worn only once in a blue moon, albeit cherished on that occasion. 'Do not,' the article warned, 'allow yourself to fall into the trap of miscategorising an item and treating it inappropriately'. The adored t-shirt: it was cheap and cheerful and has served its purpose. Don't succumb to clutter by letting it linger beyond its natural life. And the cherished jacket, last worn last year: don't recycle it because it's not worn frequently enough – its time will come again. The message was both clear and transferable: the Wardrobe Theory of Friendship was born.

How does the theory translate to real life? On a summer holiday, that couple whom you meet on day one and spend every day at the pool with and every evening in the bar together. The colleague with whom you spend many focused weeks or months, trying to navigate your way hour upon hour through work projects and politics, and dissecting the day over coffee and lunch. The mums and dads you look forward to seeing at the school gate and chatting with about everything and nothing. When the thread that holds you together drops away, what remains? Is there a friendship that endures beyond the holiday, the project or the children? If so, wonderful! They join the steadfast ranks of the winter-jumper section, which outlasts the t-shirts by years, and may even succeed to the rank of leather belt or classic handbag. And if the daily chats and phone calls dry up as swiftly as the holiday tan fades? This is fine too: simply recognise them as perfect summer t-shirts, who were exactly what you needed for the time that you were important to each other; you shouldn't be forced into remaining in each other's lives for longer than you naturally would.

Is this a callous *use-'em-and-spit-'em-out* mentality? Not at all. I'm well aware that, for many, I am a summer t-shirt: no more, no less, and I'm happy with that. Life is simply not sufficiently elastic to expand to accommodate regular contact with every person I've ever met and liked. But for some, for the leather belts in my life, I know that regardless of how hectic life has become, and how long I might spend wishing that I had time for a pub lunch and a catch up with them, or a girls' weekend away, all too aware that the hamster wheel of life has no plans to release me for a little while yet, they, my beloved leather belts, will be there.

These include my best friend from school who emigrated to China and whom I see every couple of years at best. The girl with whom I spent a gap year after leaving school, exploring life as a young teacher and then traveller in Southeast Asia, and whom I now see once a year for a weekend away together to share the intimate details of what's truly occupying our hearts and minds. The colleagues and fellow board members from Pizza Hut, with whom I now meet up for 'Ex-Board Meetings' every couple of months to share successes and challenges and gin cocktails, memories and laughter. The friend I met first in the street eleven years ago after she'd immigrated to the UK and, feeling lonely but brave, set out one day determined to look for a smiling face and make a friend. All these people and many more I love unconditionally, and do not need to speak with daily to know that they'll be in my corner in a heartbeat, as I would be for them. These relationships, which I treasure like precious trophies, contain a special balance of needing and being needed; loving and being loved; trusting and respecting in equal measure, and understanding that, to each other, we truly matter. These people are my tribe.

FORMING YOUR TRIBE

> Call it a clan, call it a network, call it a tribe, call it a family: whatever you call it, whoever you are, you need one.
> – Jane Howard, American journalist, author and editor

As the sociobiologist Edward Osborne Wilson aptly identified:

> To be kept in solitude is to be kept in pain, and put on the road

to madness. A person's membership in his group – his tribe – is a large part of his identity.

The introspection and self-analysis is only one part of the picture: the part where others join you on your journey is where it starts to get really fun.

The idea of having a tribe is not merely a trend beloved of millennial vloggers, nor one belonging to distant times and distant lands where companionship and mutual support manifested themselves around evening fires and morning fishing expeditions rather than 24/7 WhatsApp groups and Instagram updates. Having a tribe is a necessity of a happy life, no matter where or when that life is lived. Your tribe is simply the people who get you, and to whom you can turn for support and friendship without explanation. They are the ones who will look to you for an explanation if you fail to call upon them for help when they can see that you're struggling. They are the ones who will hold a mirror up to you and call you out when you're being unreasonable (they will probably let you get it all off your chest first), but will be the first in line to indulge you with pity and ice-cream for an evening before kicking your sorry ass back into the game and cheering you on for round two.

So if the tribe is so important, how do you find yours? For some, collecting acquaintances and turning them into fast friends is as easy as picking up pebbles on Brighton beach. For others, the very idea of walking into a room of strangers and leaving with a few decent conversations and a couple of plans to keep in touch seems as alien as Amazon Alexa is to my grandma. The process can be as purposeful or as organic as you choose.

TRIBE GUIDE

Assess what you need in a tribe. For you, it may be a small but close group of trusted friends and advisors. Or you might prefer a wider range of acquaintances that you're able to call upon when needed (provided you're just as available for them). As a Tribe Guide, here are some suggestions for the people you might like to include in yours...

Love and Friendship

- This may or may not mean family. Whether they're your family by blood or by choice, don't take these people for granted. Make time for them and strengthen the ties that already exist. In terms of the Wardrobe Theory of Friendship, they are the reliable leather belts and the warm coats made to last. Treasure them.

- Become someone's family: loneliness is a growing global problem. With befriending programmes to bring friendship and caring to the elderly, and shared living concepts and apps to bring like-minded people of all ages together, it is not necessary to accept loneliness as an inescapable status quo.[1]

Health and Fitness

- Joining the gym or taking up running or swimming on your own might be brilliant for building muscle and fitness but isn't necessarily the best way to build up relationships. Joining a team or exercise class, from bowls to mixed netball, is easy (whatever you might tell yourself, there *is* an activity that you can join), and group exercise such as boot camps or parkrun[2] are an incredible way to work out together in any weather. You can build strong ties, whether through the pull-ups that you do using each other's body weight, the tips, advice and encouragement that you share, or the post-workout breakfasts and dinners that you can enjoy together.[3]

- Whether your tribe member is a workout buddy or a trainer, there's a space around the campfire for that person who keeps you motivated and reminds you to look after yourself, particularly on the occasions when your own priorities are unclear or forgotten.

Work

- Just as it can be easy to let your work define you, it can be even more challenging when others allow your work to define you, and judge it slightly wrongly. This seat is for a person who has your back professionally: they work with you, or give you sound advice from their perspective, and are a fantastic sounding board when you're worried that you might be too close to the picture to see beyond the brushstrokes.

- It's not easy to build meaningful relationships from one computer screen to another. Connect for real. Whether it's a meeting spent walking around the block rather than sitting around a table, a companionable lunch break, or a drink after work, make time to connect and really get to know the person behind the role.

- Seek out a mentor from elsewhere in your organisation or from some other field altogether. Whether that person is senior or junior to you, a different perspective on the same fact pattern can yield great insights.

- Build your network: my work tribe includes members of my team and trusted friends and colleagues, global leaders and front-line colleagues within the company, counterparts in other markets, general counsel from other businesses and former colleagues now in new roles. The richness of their combined wisdom is an immeasurable benefit to me, and I value each one of them enormously.

- Consider and plan for your occasional or emergency tribe: return the recruiter's call, even if only to recommend a friend. Have coffee with the consultant. Hear out the salesperson. You never know when it'll be you who needs them, so show them the courtesy you hope to see extended to you one day.

Society

- Give something back. We all value having a helping hand available when we most need it. Whether a knowledgeable advisor at Citizens Advice when we have a question that flummoxes us; or the volunteer marshal pointing the way, handing out water and dispensing shouts of encouragement as we run our first (or fiftieth) big race; or the people doing whatever they can to fundraise for the charity that doesn't particularly resonate with us, as we've never suffered that particular hardship. Until one sickening day, it starts to mean a great deal... If it feels good to be supported, it feels even better to be needed and to be able to help. Society needs people on both sides of the equation, so take the time to consider some of the ways you can step from one side to the other. (See Useful Addresses, for some suggestions on how to give something back.)

- Some of the happiest people I know are not the ones with

the biggest bank balances, or the wonderful spouse and 2.4 offspring. They're the ones who do something that has no direct tangible benefit to themselves at all. The friend who is an emergency foster carer for children in dire need; the colleague who leads a Brownies pack and fundraises tirelessly; the angel who spends her weekends visiting elderly people who are all on their own but for her regular visits for coffee and cake and a chat that brings a bubble of light and happiness from the outside world into their lives for a while. It feels good to do good. And it's a great reminder that what might seem like the weight of the world to us when it's 11.30pm and it's been a long day and we should probably simply go to bed is actually not that bad when viewed through the lens of a chirpy nine-year-old, or a war veteran, or a child who arrives in temporary care with only the soiled clothes she's been wearing all week.

- Serve as a charitable trustee; volunteer your time; mentor, lead, coach, befriend. Do good. Feel good.

Avoid the temptation to look only to people likely to cheer you on and support your ways of thinking to form your tribe. Just as important, perhaps more so, are the people who see things differently, and who will be prepared to point out the opportunities and hazards that you might have missed. The importance of this will be explored in more detail in Chapter 9.

A FRIEND IN NEED: BE ONE, SUPPORT ONE

In February and March 2018, I experienced one of the most intense and demanding periods of my work life for some years. I was leading the European Legal Team at KFC when the company went through a period of crisis on an unprecedented scale. The control that I had over my life – where I would be working that day; whom I would spend time with; when I would eat and sleep – was removed with one swift blow. (The background to this crisis will be explored in Part III.) In its place was a rollercoaster of crises and negotiations and ad hoc meetings and sleeplessness and stress, through which I careered at breakneck speed, just barely hanging on. For one forty-eight-hour period, I'd forget to make time to consume anything but coffee. For another, I'd notice that the sun had risen and I had yet to stumble into bed and close my eyes on the day before. The regular payments that I cherish making into my various friendship banks ground to a halt: this was the time to rely on the funds well invested. Now more than ever, I needed my tribe.

Lining up the right support at the right time is certainly on the critical list. There's an inclination for many in-house lawyers, for example, cognisant of budgetary constraints, to try to take on as much work as they can themselves. Yet there comes a point when managing on your own flips 180° from being heroic to being idiotic. With a small but strong legal team, all of whom were keen to do whatever they could to offer support, roles needed to be considered carefully and allocated wisely. My team rallied round and stepped up to the plate, making sure that everything that needed to be done to keep all of the balls in the air was done and, through regular calls and messages, we continued to operate as a cohesive unit, albeit a unit under pressure.

Internal resources were finite, however. External resources were somewhat more elastic. So with my team retaining focus on supporting KFC across Europe and managing business as usual outside the crisis, additional support would need to come from elsewhere. In the early days of the crisis, when the ever-changing list of tasks to be undertaken morphed and grew, and the supply of conscious hours in which to accomplish them dwindled, I seized half an hour alone in a meeting room to make a call to a lawyer from one of KFC's panel of law firms upon which it relied most regularly. We talked through my thoughts on where we currently stood, and what I believed our options to be. We discussed and debated and reached agreement and then, wonderfully, she said the words: 'Give me a couple of hours: I'll meet you at your office.' I knew straight away that the burden was shared, and it felt wonderful.

Don't let the fire take hold while you debate which fire extinguisher to use

Asking for help too early in a crisis can feel like admitting to weakness, or giving up where you should persevere and succeed on your own. Leave it too late, though, and it might seem impossible to wrench yourself away from firefighting in order to bring someone else up to speed and teach them how to work the hoses. Instead, consider the options early, and be realistic. Optimism at this stage might leave you underprepared later on.

My colleagues and I spoke early with independent consultants. With an experienced but impartial viewpoint, they were tasked with delving into the situation and helping us to identify how and why the problems had begun. Alongside this root-cause analysis, they helped us to determine and map out the most efficient strategy to navigate a path through the initial crunch.

My home support network of family and au pair made sure that life there continued as close to normal as possible, albeit without me in it very much. The area of my world's biggest hit, though, was my own physical and mental health. I had carefully constructed my life to ensure that each sphere had just enough focus, including the precious hours that I had to myself each week. For some people, it's the time spent kicking their shoes off and zoning out on the sofa with a glass of wine and Netflix, requiring little conscious thought, that's most important to them. For others, it's an early night, or a game of football with friends. For me, it was a morning training session in the park, with about thirty people similarly wet and muddy and doing their best to keep up with the instructions being bellowed at them by the instructor.[4] Being able to suspend all mental effort in order to put everything into the physical effort of simply following instructions for an hour, and feeling an exhausted elation as the instruction finally comes to begin the stretches – this is what keeps me feeling good, and feeling sane.

During the KFC distribution crisis, however, getting to the 6.30am weekday classes was sometimes impossible when I'd returned from work at 4am that morning. And the 10am Sunday class clashed with an early start in the office. Sitting in the office one Saturday night, as the hours of cerebral effort left me drained, and the lack of physical activity left me feeling restless, Paul, my fitness instructor messaged me:

Paul: *Where have you been? I feel like I've not seen you this week!*

Me: *It's been an interesting one for me… Google KFC news… Seriously need a workout!!*

Paul: *They're out of chicken!! Will you be training tomorrow or just working hard?*

Me: *Need to get to the office v early so going to have to miss it unfortunately*

Paul: *How early? I could train you at 7 if you like. See you there.*

Afterwards, we had another exchange:

> Me: *Thanks a million for this. Today's a bit of a s••• storm, so you set me up well for it. Ta!*

> Paul: *You're welcome. I thought it would do you good. Hope work goes ok. It will calm down soon.*

Throughout the crisis, I rarely missed a workout: the group sessions gave me a blast of companionship, from friends who worked as police officers dealing with the knife crime epidemic gripping the city to a director in a hospitality company with stories of boozy lunches and whole day brunches – stories that kept me laughing and grounded and conscious that there is a great deal more to life than chicken and chips. And on the days that getting to the classes was an impossibility, I trained until I wanted to vomit from sheer exertion with a trainer who had taken time out of his day to fulfil his role in my tribe, and who asked for nothing in return.

We can be pretty poor at asking for help when we need it. Sometimes, though, it's when we're most in need of support that we're least able to step back and accurately assess what it is that we need. It's then that we rely most heavily on our support network: our tribe.

KEYS FOR FINDING YOUR TRIBE

- Map out what you believe your support network, or your tribe, should look like. Wherever there are gaps, think carefully about how best to fill them so that you can surround yourself with incredible people. The people I choose as members of my tribe (and the people I choose to hire into my team at work) are all demonstrably stronger than me in at least one area: celebrate and learn from the strengths of others.

- Minimise your blind spots. In a work situation, this might mean practising crisis situations and identifying the areas of weakness that could prove disastrous in a genuine crisis. In other spheres too, discuss and understand what Plan B will look like, and who and what you might need to ensure it is a viable alternative.

- Be sure to keep the friendship bank topped up: if you don't pay enough into it, whether through time, compassion or other support, you cannot expect to draw down on it when you're in need of credit. Invest in your relationships, and offer support: everybody needs to feel that they're not alone, and that somebody has their back.

- Accept help: don't be too proud to accept an offer of kindness that has been extended. Feeling needed feels good, and can strengthen relationships.

- Being a supportive member of somebody's tribe is not the same as being a free resource to be used with abandon. There needs to be reciprocity. If you're carrying them when times are good, they'll be drowning you when things get bad. Life is short and our time should be wisely spent.

6. Understand The Background

Nobody realised at the time that the events of Valentine's Day 2018 would mark the beginning of the single biggest crisis in the forty-five-year history of the UK Kentucky Fried Chicken business. That as the country was waking up, the restaurants being unlocked and the daily pre-opening checks completed, the KFC distribution crisis was already inevitable.

I suspect my Valentine's Day had every bit as exciting a start as it did for any other middle-aged, married, working mother of two. There was a card from my husband, Adam. There was always a card from my husband, ever since the disastrous Valentine's Day in my tiny attic flat at law school, when Adam had visited for the weekend. He'd arrived in a foul mood, having taken on the M1 at the wrong time, and had quite clearly given no thought to the practicalities of procuring a half decent bunch of flowers and a card twelve hours into what purported to be the most romantic day of the year. We'd argued about spaghetti. It's hard to imagine quite how you could argue about spaghetti. The issue was that I had a plastic spatula, and Adam was adamant that preparing spaghetti with anything other than a wooden spoon was entirely impossible. It seems silly now. It seemed bloody ridiculous then, so I decided to divert attention from the inadequacies of my student kitchen by opening the card that he had left on the side, next to half a dozen gasping carnations.

The card had two bears embossed on the front, so that they seemed to loom out from the background towards me. And underneath, the words 'I bearly wuw wou'. There were many levels upon which the card offended me. Suddenly, the very last card in the petrol station had relegated the appropriate fabric for a spatula to a minor detail in the grander scheme of our relationship, and the remainder of the day passed in a blur of burned spaghetti, and very lively debate. Perhaps unsurprisingly, I have never received a card with talking bears on it again. So this year, there was a card, a lovely card, and a beautiful bunch of flowers, whose stems I carefully trimmed before arranging them with neither skill nor artistic flair in a vase.

STARTING OUT WITH KFC

'I genuinely cannot think of anything worse,' one of my oldest friends, Rena, gasped when I first joined the company in early 2007, and told her that I'd be kicking off my career by working in one of the London KFC restaurants. 'Is there anything you could do to get out of it? You're a lawyer Sarah – not a cook!' And, although I love her dearly, she had entirely missed the point.

Every new joiner at KFC, whether employed in a restaurant, in the field as an area or regional coach or trainer, or in the head office (known as the Restaurant Support Centre or the 'RSC'), spends time training in a restaurant when they first arrive. It makes sense: the whole point of KFC is to prepare and sell chicken and chips. If anyone in the company didn't know how to do that properly, it would highlight an unhealthy disconnect between the individual and the core business, and a lack of genuine understanding of what the business is really about. Thus everyone begins by getting to grips with the roles that the majority of KFC's employees perform every day.

I earned my wings in the flagship restaurant that stood on the fringes of Leicester Square in central London. I had spent only two days in the RSC, meeting the team, finding my feet and getting kitted out with my uniform when, on day three, I set off for my restaurant training. As I sat on the train heading into the city, my only concern was whether, on the way back that evening, I'd smell so powerfully of fried food that my fellow passengers would give me a wide berth. The very idea of anyone travelling out of London in rush hour being given plenty of space is as laughable as it is wonderful. I was looking forward to the experience.

From my first babysitting job aged eleven to pulling on my red shirt and baseball cap that morning, I had stitched together a colourful and varied patchwork quilt of different jobs and roles. Evenings and weekends spent chatting and daydreaming on the supermarket checkout paid for my first car. And backpacking trips, charity bike rides and the deposit on the first house of my own were financed through various part-time positions. Other roles served different purposes: I simply never understood how it was possible to post a letter in Cornwall on Monday, and have it drop through a letter box in Hull on Tuesday, so I replied to a request for seasonal workers to support the Royal Mail with the Christmas post, and engineered tasks in as many different areas as possible so that I could see how it all slotted together (a process that I still find pretty incredible). Being welcomed behind the counter of the KFC restaurant that morning and instructed to tie my hair back and scrub my hands before learning how to take crates of fresh, raw chicken joints, hand bread them, pressure cook them, and finally pass them across the counter packed into the iconic red cardboard buckets may well have been a hellish proposition for Rena, but it felt pretty cool to me.

I've silently eye-rolled at children's arguments against learning their multiplication tables: *you're not given weekly tables tests as an adult, so what's the point in learning them as a child?* This seems to be the same rationale employed, whether consciously or subconsciously, by any of us who focus only on the direct route from studying A to a career in B, and not on the numerous factors that go into making us better equipped for when we eventually arrive at B, our chosen destination. There are many lessons that can be picked up along the way to improve the efficiency or enjoyment of the passage.

In the KFC context, understanding how the team is recruited and managed, how the equipment is used, how the restaurant manager performs her hourly checks, what the proper cleaning procedures are and the myriad other details that make up a day in the life of the restaurant team is important. This necessary context for my role, as the company's legal advisor, impacted the ways in which my team and I delivered the support that the business needed. New initiatives and processes that would work brilliantly in a single restaurant might prove unworkable or financially or practically unrealistic when implemented across a market of almost one thousand.

The general counsel of another international restaurant chain told me once that he believed one of the common character flaws in lawyers is their arrogance: many truly believe that there's no job in the world that they couldn't do brilliantly, it's simply that they've chosen to alight upon the law. Spending time with brilliant people who excel in an entirely different discipline, such as the twenty-six-year-old restaurant manager who has responsibility for running a £2 million business, for hiring, training, motivating and retaining teams of up to sixty people, and for dealing with the full spectrum of employee and customer issues, face to face, every day (and often night) of the week, is a good way to challenge that belief. And watching the speed with which a skilled cook takes the raw chicken, washes it and expertly breads every piece by hand, tucking the wing back into itself so that it doesn't get burned or broken in the cooking process, twisting the joint of the drumstick to be sure that the skin doesn't come loose when being pressure cooked before patiently repeating the process more slowly so that I could learn and follow: this was an excellent reminder of how important it is to have a rainbow of talented people working together, each expert in their own field.

As people around England trimmed the stems of their Valentine's bouquets, delivered to their place of work for additional impact and Brownie points, I sat down for a chat and a bucket of freshly cooked chicken with two of the UK KFC franchisees in one of their south London restaurants. We took a walk around the kitchen, chatting with the team and picking up any questions or requests that they had (such as, when are the new uniforms going to be rolled out to the whole system? Were team members able to complete the online GDPR training module?), before sitting down with Shahaz and Saf, the two brothers who own and operate the restaurant, to talk chicken. Shahaz and Saf are second-generation franchisees, and own several KFC restaurants across south-east England. Their parents started the KFC franchise business when they were small boys, and they'd help out in the restaurant after school. For family treats, they'd take a big bucket of original recipe chicken and a few pots of gravy, and sit together catching up and sharing the minutiae of their day. Their friends have asked them why they now put everything into the family business when they could have walked away and started something new of their own, something other than chicken. Their response is pretty simple: they love the food. They love the company that they've built up over generations. And they love the brand.

Shahaz and Saf's story is not unique. KFC first arrived in the UK in Preston, Lancashire, in May 1965. This restaurant, the first American fast-food-chain restaurant in the country, was owned by Ray Allen, an established caterer in the area, and the first KFC franchisee outside of the United States. Over the next ten years, Ray expanded KFC significantly, building his business to 400 restaurants across the UK. By 2018, there were over 900 KFC restaurants in the UK, with fifty owned and operated by KFC itself, and the remainder by thirty-two franchisees, many of whom are second-generation business owners. The KFC brand was woven into the fabric and history of these families even before many of the sons and daughters were ready to stake their claim on the family business. And as the franchisees have grown up with the company, so too has the company grown up, developed and evolved with them.

WHY CHANGE WHAT'S NOT BROKEN?

For over a decade, the UK KFC business had relied upon Bidvest Logistics as the main distributor of stock to each of the UK KFC restaurants. Produce from over 200 suppliers of food, packaging, uniforms and sundries were delivered into the three Bidvest distribution centres in Manchester, Oxfordshire and Hertfordshire. Huge, sprawling warehouses, they were used by a number of food service businesses to ensure that shops, restaurants and pubs across the south of England were supplied with all that they needed to trade.

The system and the process worked. And yet... Who doesn't ask themselves whether good could be better? Or whether better can be best? Which business doesn't question whether there is perhaps a better way of doing what they're already doing?

Whether they could be more efficient, have a more positive impact on the lives of their teams and customers, or on the environment? Who hasn't looked at advances in technology and questioned whether their own systems and processes could benefit from a technological jump start? KFC certainly asked itself these questions.

Looking at the changes that the brand had gone through in the last decade, it's pretty clear that it had no intention of standing still. Whether setting new standards in animal welfare and sustainable packaging, launching a KFC degree and apprenticeship scheme, or bringing a food donation programme to the majority of its restaurants, the company constantly sought to improve its products, to bring greater benefits to its employees and the communities and the environment in which it operates, and to innovate so as continue to be a modern and relevant brand.

It should be no surprise that the company's distributor also came under scrutiny. KFC manages the UK supply chain for the benefit of the restaurants that it owns and operates itself, and also the restaurants that are owned and operated by its franchisees. As a global franchisor, it is understandable that KFC has, through the franchise agreements that it has with each of its UK franchisees, retained the right to unilaterally take the decisions that it, in its experience, deems to be in the best interests of the KFC system as a whole. And yet, in practice, it doesn't operate like that. From the inside, KFC operates as a democracy, with the voice of the franchisees sought and listened to. As owners and operators of over 90 per cent of the KFC estate, it stands to reason that the franchisees will have significant insights into what works and what doesn't. Any decisions made by the company are made hand in hand with its franchisees.

So when, in October 2016, discussions around the right distributor for the brand began to ramp up a gear, people from several areas of the company and the franchise network were involved. DHL Logistics, the UK logistics arm of the German-owned global distribution and logistics group, Deutsche Post, and Quick Service Logistics (or 'QSL') had submitted a joint pitch. Their proposition was based on the model that QSL had been operating successfully in Germany and across Europe for numerous companies, including the Burger King and KFC businesses in Germany and Poland since 2008. QSL would provide the interface between the individual KFC restaurants and the suppliers of the goods. Orders would be received from the restaurants by QSL, and QSL would manage the process of transforming the thousands of bespoke requests received each week into pick-lists to be used by the DHL team in the warehouse.

DHL was to operate from a new, state of the art 180,000 square-foot distribution centre in Rugby. Sitting squarely within what is known as the 'golden triangle' of the UK warehousing world, Rugby is within just a few hours' reach of most of Britain's major cities via the M1, M6 and M42 motorways that surround it. For this reason, it is common practice for companies to locate their sole distribution centre in the area. Working together, DHL and QSL promised to set a new (and KFC assumed higher) benchmark for delivering fresh products to KFC in a sustainable way.[1] The warehouse would always be stocked to an appropriate level, with deliveries of goods arriving into it every hour of every day of the week, in response to the orders placed by QSL. And the hundreds of wheeled cages, constantly on the move in the distribution centre, would be filled with products picked to order and loaded into the fleet of DHL vehicles that would be standing waiting.

The Rugby distribution centre and the employees within it would bear the red and yellow DHL branding, as would the fleet of trucks, with frozen, chilled and ambient compartments, waiting to be packed exclusively with products to be used in and sold from KFC restaurants. This would be bread and butter to DHL, who were well used to providing a similar service to other British companies, such as J D Wetherspoon and Sainsbury's. QSL would invoice the franchise or KFC-owned restaurants for the stock delivered to each of them, and so the cycle would continue.

Understand the intention

Any problem can have numerous solutions. When you're trying to get to the bottom of why someone might be doing something, or why they're doing it in a particular way, first, understand the outcome that they're trying to achieve. You will then have the opportunity to support by proposing different, perhaps better ways of getting to the desired outcome rather than simply helping with their chosen method.

For example, if you see a friend struggling to plan the most efficient bus route from A to B, you could help them to plan their connections as efficiently as possible, before getting into your car and waving them goodbye as you drive directly to B and wait for them there. You're unlikely to be thanked for this help though.

Whilst neither the goal nor the result of the move was to cut the cost of distribution, the enhanced level of service offered and the innovations proposed were compelling. One of the main attractions of the DHL and QSL proposal was that the service would be provided solely for KFC. KFC was used to receiving a shared service, with both vehicles and people within the distribution chain also servicing different brands. Whilst this was not unusual within the sector, it meant that the sense of pride amongst the buying, warehouse and fleet teams in being a part of the KFC family was challenging to foster and maintain, and the difficulties in conforming to the specific stringent standards demanded by KFC were at times insurmountable. Having a non-shared service was hugely attractive as, it was promised, it would enable greater consistency of process and people, and greater efficiency throughout the system. With additional promises made by the new partnership around quality, efficiency and innovation of service, sustainability, and reductions in emissions from the logistics network to a net of zero over the period of the contract, the die was cast. In June 2017, the decision was made to move away from Bidvest.

It seems almost too obvious to say, but the decision was not taken lightly. Rather it was the result of many months of tender submissions, discussions, pitches and reviews by a cross-functional KFC and franchisee group on behalf of the wider KFC business. And so began nine months of the KFC UK supply chain team and a working group from DHL and QSL mapping out what the transition from Bidvest to the newly formed partnership would look like. A number of jobs at the Bidvest distribution centres would inevitably be lost, but the net number of new roles created would exceed that figure.

There were complexities of course. KFC UK insists on sourcing its chicken on the bone exclusively from British and Irish farms, and having it delivered fresh into a network of almost a thousand restaurants every day. There is very little margin for error. Raw chicken storage and transportation is heavily regulated: the negative impact of getting it wrong, and allowing sub-standard chicken to make it through to customers' plates (or buckets), must of course be avoided at all costs, so KFC also imposes even tougher standards than mandated by UK law in the processing of its chicken. According to a supply chain, logistics and transport consultant quoted in the *Financial Times* at the time, it is very unusual to use fresh rather than frozen chicken in the quick service industry: the law provides for very specific temperatures within which poultry must be kept, and KFC has quality expectations even more stringent than that. This naturally adds greater complexity into the supply chain.2

The scale of the change was intimidating, but the KFC steering group, headed by the general manager, took comfort from the fact that DHL was a global logistics company with a strong track record, and QSL was expert in the technology behind the process. With both of them picking up the reins and leading KFC through the change, KFC was surely in excellent hands.

When seeing really is believing...

Never rely entirely on theory when you can roll your sleeves up and put something into practice for yourself. The difference between discussing or reading about something and seeing it with your own eyes is vast.

A friend once ordered a beautiful hand-knitted jumper over the internet, for a surprisingly reasonable price. When it arrived, it was clear that the description had been accurate. It looked just as it did in the picture: the colour was just as vivid as she had hoped, and the quality as good.

What was also immediately apparent, however, was the fact

that the size 'm' had been intended to fit a medium-sized doll, rather than a medium-sized woman. Her own assumptions had prevented her from digging deeper and asking the questions to which the seller had assumed she already knew the answers.

Take every opportunity to check that your assumptions are correct.

A lawyer from KFC's in-house team stepped in to support the project team through months of contract negotiation and, by the end of the process, there was no doubt among the three parties where each of their obligations lay, and who was responsible for what. The agreement was, according to a supply chain expert, the best distribution agreement he'd ever seen, with protections for KFC that he'd never before found to be included in a contract of this type. Nor, as it transpired, that he would ever see again. All that remained was for the changeover from old to new to progress smoothly. Initial hiccups would be inevitable – nobody and nothing is perfect – but the strong expectation by all parties was that all would be well.

Like most people in the KFC business, I had no idea on that Valentine's Day morning that the long-awaited distributor changeover had already begun to go horribly wrong.

As we've seen, there is plenty that we can do to build courage and resilience, and ensure that we are well placed for whatever life might toss our way. However, being well prepared does not mean that the path ahead will not feel challenging and potentially exhausting, terrifying and almost overwhelming at times. What it does mean is that you can feel confident that you will get through it.

So how exactly will you get through it? Well, you'll start by reading Part III...

KEYS FOR TURNING THEORY INTO REALITY

- **Theory is excellent, in theory. To truly get to grips with something to see how it works, step through the theoretical and into the practical: logically, putting a nappy on a baby is easy if you follow the diagram on the pack. Factor in a wriggling baby, time pressure and pee halfway through, and chaos will ensue. Some of these things you'll only know if you try it out.**

- If you believe that you understand a situation well (your job? your company? yourself?), step into somebody else's shoes and take another look from that angle. A dining table that looks polished and slick from the top may look unfinished and rough from underneath. Roll your sleeves up; get your hands dirty; open your eyes.

- Seize every opportunity to build relationships and strengthen friendships: you never know when you'll need to rely on them, and it will be too late then to begin from scratch. Time spent getting to know people from different areas of expertise or walks of life to you is rarely if ever time wasted: it's an opportunity to learn more than you already know, or to share some of the knowledge that you've picked up along the way. Or ideally both.

- Welcome diverse viewpoints: life is not binary. It's unlikely you have the sole correct answer to many topics. It has been said that there are at least fifty shades of grey...

- When you have time available, use it wisely. When you have little or no time available, use it strategically.

Part III
Survive the Crises

A crisis: as defined in the *Oxford English Dictionary*, this is a 'time of intense difficulty or danger', when 'a difficult or important decision must be made'. It is not limited to the office, or working hours. It is not possible to insist that crises be kept safely separate from the domestic sphere. On our return from a fantastic family holiday in Cape Verde one year, the slight feeling of travel sickness that uncharacteristically bothered all but the youngest member of the family soon turned out to be salmonella. A crisis? Yes, most definitely. But did we handle it as such, ensuring that each of the stages set out below were followed, and regular, clear lines of communication with employers, schools, family doctor and the local authority established? Next time...

Like a chip pan fire that takes hold when you've stepped away from the hob for a moment and your focus has briefly wandered to other things, a crisis can leap and spread insidiously from one area to the next to the next, until everything that it touches – and it touches everything – is engulfed.

Part III

Survive the Crisis

7. Spotting The Footprints In The Butter

Q: How can you tell if there's an elephant in your fridge?

A: There are footprints in the butter.

Working through the possible maths on the Q&A above, it's clear that it is in fact excellent advice. Commercial fridges can be cavernous places, and with some breeds of elephant, such as the Borneo pygmy elephant, whose calf measures a teeny weeny and easily missed 30cm when first born, it's not so hard to visualise dozens of them pottering around the 60,000-square-foot chiller at the DHL distribution centre in Rugby without immediately being spotted. So, if the fridge floor were to be liberally buttered, following the string of little disc impressions pressed into it by the elephant calves as they shuttle under shelving and play amongst the pallets might be very effective in tracking them down, or indeed in arousing the suspicion that there might be an elephant infestation in the fridge in the first place.

Alternative, and, potentially, better methods for identifying the issue and managing the situation through to a successful resolution also exist however, and will be explored throughout the following pages.

THE CRISIS BEGINS

During the KFC distribution crisis, the footprints had been gently pressed into the butter for a little while before the first hidden elephants were spotted. Well before the planned changeover date from the incumbent distributor to the new, a test period was scheduled. KFC's sister brand, Taco Bell, had only twenty-three restaurants in the UK, and relied on the same supply chain and distributor as KFC. With an entirely different product range to KFC, but one that also encompassed ambient, chilled and frozen products, it was selected by the project team as a good, contained group with which to conduct the trial.

The process was not without incident, but as issues arose, the working group flagged them, discussed them, and agreed upon a fix or a sensible alternative workaround. Business continued as usual for Taco Bell, and the changeover day for the KFC system drew closer. The scale of the undertaking was colossal. At that time, the UK KFC system consumed 19 million cases of over 200 different product lines a year, and orders received from over 900 restaurants eagerly awaiting deliveries were packed up and sent out to stores country-wide, from Jersey in the English Channel, right up to Elgin in northern Scotland.

The teams working in the restaurants had been briefed numerous times over the previous weeks and months, and knew to expect new drivers who were unfamiliar with the routes and who might need a little extra support and understanding while they got to grips with delivering to KFC. As a company, KFC's focus on training and development, both functional and personal, is strong. People are very used to welcoming new joiners on board, and investing time to draw upon the raw potential, coaching and training until they're achieving all that they'd hoped to or more. The teams were ready for a few bumps in the road.

Over at the Rugby depot, things were not going smoothly. The relationship between QSL and DHL was a new one. They had no combined memory of lessons learned together the hard way to draw upon. Each was experienced in their area, but they hadn't previously worked as a partnership, and the easy interface between the companies and the people working within them was yet to be established. The DHL teams in the depot were new and enthusiastic, but their enthusiasm wasn't quite sufficient to compensate for lack of experience. And there was barely any window to learn on the job. Deliveries were arriving at the depot on 50-foot articulated trucks fresh from chicken farms across the UK and Ireland, salad producers across Europe and packaging manufacturers as far afield as China and India, at a rate of up to three vehicles every hour. With up to forty trucks arriving at the depot each day, and forty pallets to be offloaded from each, the process simply had to be smooth, and the operators efficient and clear.

Temporary sticking plasters that would work just fine in most situations cannot work in a colossal 180,000-square-foot warehouse, where the available loading and unloading space is disappearing by the hour under hundreds of pallets and cages left there for just a minute, and being blocked off from the route to their proper homes by the hundreds of new pallets in a similar state of homelessness. It takes surprisingly little time for disaster to clamp itself resolutely around a situation, when a large team of people with the best of intentions but little experience assume that requests for 'COB' will be satisfied by corn cobs, rather than by 'chicken on the bone', and that leaving something in the wrong place for 'just a minute' will truly be just a minute. After a few short hours of confusion, the rot of gridlock has set in. The routes from unloading bays to chiller and freezer are impassable; the possibility of finding the right products to load back into the cages is diminishing and the route for the loaded cages to be propelled back to the vehicles waiting to deliver them to the restaurants is being subsumed by pallets and cages left there for just a minute.

It would take nerves of steel not to be daunted by the sight of four acres of newly erected distribution warehouse, serviced by a slowing army of trucks inching into the yard, pregnant with stock, but with neither space nor operators available to enable safe delivery. The drivers, captive in their cabs, were wearily calling back to their bases: having driven across Europe, they were now faced with interminable delays in unloading the vehicles in front of them. They waited for hours to enter the depot, with limited time in which it would be possible for them to unload before they'd have to make the call to turn and head back to their own point of loading. And yet, they could not do that either: after nine hours behind the wheel, the drivers needed at least nine hours to rest before they could safely and legally begin the return journey. And the drivers of the vehicles scheduled to head out to each of the KFC restaurants, fully loaded with supplies, were also caught up in the tangle: parked alongside the articulated trucks, their own tachographs measuring the hours spend idling on Rugby's roads, their own minds were turning to where they'd sleep that evening.

For the hoteliers of Rugby, business flourished. For the KFC restaurant managers noting with increasing concern the dwindling supply of fresh produce, it did not.

The queue of trucks into the depot snaked around the roads and roundabouts of the town like a giant arrow pointing: *Look! This way!* Before, there was nothing but footprints, but now, there are thousands upon thousands of elephants to be seen, hidden in plain sight: standing defiantly in the butter.

SOUND THE ALARM

Perhaps the most important step in responding to a crisis is recognising that it is a crisis. This is not the time for retrospection: how did we get here? Whose fault was it? Does anyone think (do I think?) that any of the blame should be laid at my door? There is a time and a place for that. This is not it.

This is the time for making sure that every man, woman and stakeholder who needs to know is made fully aware that all is not well. This is the time for digging – quick and deep – to get a good understanding of what the issue is: a static question with an organic answer. At every point, it's important to know what the current answer is, and then to keep an open mind as to what the answer is for the next hour, and the next day, and beyond. And this is the time to assemble your tribe.

The business leaders or key players when all is well might not be the right people to pick for your crisis tribe. Ideally, you'd have planned this in advance, and will have a readily available contact list of the people to draft in to help in a situation such as this. But if you didn't, plan now. Call on everyone who might need to know or might be able to support. This crisis response tribe too will need to be organic for several reasons: matters progress, knowledge deepens and needs change. Plus people tire. An enthusiastic sprint to respond to a call to arms is fantastic on day one. But by day twelve, how much enthusiasm and clear-headedness will remain?

PRACTICAL STEPS TO TAKE

One of the first steps we took in responding to the KFC crisis was to create a crisis hub. All of the meeting rooms on the

ground floor of the office were commandeered, and recon-
figured as the nerve centre for the crisis response. TV screens
showed sales figures for each of the restaurants, hour by hour,
so we could track which restaurants were trading and what
volumes were being sold. The facilities teams and the PAs
made sure that there was food and drink available for those
working flat out in the crisis hub, plus a stash of ProPlus and
painkillers always close at hand. A dimly lit meeting room
was prepared, blinds drawn, carpet littered with oversized bean
bags and comfy sofas, with an array of toiletries and spare t-
shirts for the people who would be working through the night
and into the next day.

> It is amazing what you can accomplish if you do not care who
> gets the credit.
> – Harry S. Truman, thirty-third president of the United States

Everybody had a job to do, and did it with utter efficiency and
minimal fuss. A question about corporate structure was met with a
full response and printed reports in a matter of minutes. My request
for a telephone battery pack was outstanding for only moments
before my phone was being stripped of its case and clipped into a
chunky and fully charged replacement. Phone calls made at 3am
were answered. My role, at the heart of the crisis team, was to establish where we stood from a commercial point of view, and pull
together and manage all of the different strands that would, if well
handled, ensure our position only improved rather than deterio-
rated. This touched upon anything and everything: carefully drafting and laying down the parameters for our communications
(whether with internal teams, franchisees or the outside world);
holding town hall Q&A sessions with franchise partners who were
understandably keen to know what was being done; strategising
and planning the operational steps that would mitigate the situa-

tion, and commercial negotiations that would eventually enable all parties to move on from it further down the line. Importantly, it also meant ensuring that the teams around me felt reassured and confident that we were headed boldly in the right direction, even if we weren't currently in the right place.

With the vehicle tracking systems that had been promised to KFC not yet up and running, we needed a way to let the restaurants know when their deliveries would be arriving. The usual delivery windows had been abandoned: instead, everybody simply accepted that the trucks would turn up whenever they got there. Restaurant teams took it in turns to remain in the restaurants, bundled up in sleeping bags throughout the night, while the night shift in the office tracked all of the vehicles as they left the depot and arrived at each restaurant, calling ahead to let the next restaurant know when their delivery should be expected. The walls were papered with charts and lists and maps and routes, and mugs of hot coffee were passed hand to hand like a blessing.

Leave your ego at the door

You're in no doubt at all that you are up to your oxters in a crisis. The crisis response tribe has been assembled, and as the storm keeps changing direction and intensity, so must you. Follow any action plans and protocols you've prepared in advance, but be dynamic so that you can add to them or flex away as the issue snowballs, and your understanding deepens. Here, real grit comes into play.

Whatever the circumstances, as jackets are being shrugged off and sleeves rolled up, all egos should be left at the door.

This is not about any of you: it's about finding a way to first stabilise and then resolve the situation. And the adventure has only just begun.

THE EYE OF THE STORM

During the KFC crisis, it felt at times like a gruesome game of whack-a-mole: as soon as one obstacle was successfully overcome, the next would tauntingly rear its head. First, the depot was gridlocked with misplaced stock. The scale of the problem was potentially overwhelming, and was an obvious colossal blocker to any real progress. The blockage was cleared (easy to sum up in four words, which belie the scale of the undertaking and the effort). Next, it became apparent that there were not enough drivers with sufficient available hours to make the deliveries to restaurants. Easily fixed: new drivers were drafted in from other parts of the DHL network and from agencies. Which led to problem number three: the new drivers were unfamiliar with the routes and the vehicles, and struggled with the complexities of the orders being delivered.

The partial fix to this problem was a by-product of a fix to another problem: the pickers were finding it impossible to locate and pick the myriad bespoke orders coming in from each of the 920 restaurants. The shelves and aisles weren't being replenished due to the gridlock at the point of unloading, which had now spread like a cancer to every corner of the depot, and the pickers had all but given up trying to find and identify the right items. The task of picking the order for one restaurant should have taken just under three quarters of an hour. It was now taking more than treble that time before being abandoned. And so, rather than focusing on removing blockers, the strategy changed, to changing the strategy.

Chicken on the bone is delivered into the restaurants fresh every day, ready to be hand breaded, piece by piece, and then pressure cooked in the restaurants. The meat can be stored in the chillers for a maximum of five days from delivery, although it is generally used within forty-eight hours. With Bidvest's last deliveries into restaurants made on Monday 12th and Tuesday 13th February, by three days after the switchover the restaurants were fast running out of chicken and salad. Most had sufficient stores of frozen and ambient stock, but without being able to prepare and cook the Original Recipe chicken on the bone, the restaurants were not permitted to open. KFC without any of the Original Recipe Kentucky Fried Chicken? No.

So a team in the crisis hub devised a core rescue pack that could be delivered as a standard package to each and every restaurant. It would enable each restaurant to serve a limited core menu, whilst remaining true to the brand – arguably truer than the standard menu, which, with Rice Boxes, Zingers, Krushems and Twister Wraps was a far cry from the Colonel's 1950s simple concept of the best chicken and fries you'd ever taste. Thus the new strategy removed the complexity of the bespoke orders from the mix, and operations in the depot became significantly easier.

A new rhythm had begun. The urgent to-do lists that had existed prior to the crisis were mothballed, waiting for a time when simply getting stock to restaurants and staying open was no longer the main focus of every mind in the business. Every person within KFC seemed to have been plucked up from their usual roles and repositioned in the place that made more sense today: strong and experienced restaurant managers and area coaches would have more impact in the depot where their familiarity with the packaged products destined for the restaurants would be a huge benefit to the newly hired pickers, who saw only oceans of boxes. Operations leaders from both the KFC-owned and franchise business made their way quickly up to Rugby. With years of experience in creating workable systems, they could be injected like anti-venom into the epicentre of the depot, their clear thinking and calm organisation spreading like ripples across a lake, bringing order and the belief that this crisis was surmountable.

Hour by hour, step by step, the behemoth that was the paralysed KFC distribution system juddered back to life.

With any challenge, allow yourself to feel daunted by it. But, before sprinting away and giving up on adulting for good, push yourself to do what you need to do to be able to properly understand what you're facing. Once you understand it, you can break it down into manageable chunks, and tackle each one, bit by bit. Remind yourself if necessary that this is simply a Bucket 2 or a Bucket 3 situation, and that you will get through it.

KEYS TO SPOTTING THE FOOTPRINTS IN THE BUTTER

- No matter how hideous the crisis, it can be broken down into manageable quarters: recognition of the crisis, navigating through the eye of the storm, closure and post mortem. Take each at a time.

- Forget the ego (or allocating the blame).

- It may not be as straightforward as you first imagine, and your approach may need to be multifarious. Keep learning, and keep communicating as openly, honestly, clearly and frequently as is appropriate.

- Be dynamic: what's right for now might not be right for the next hour or day, so be prepared to give your all to a course of action, only to drop it like a hot potato and begin again on a different tack with just as much vigour.

- Firefighting may well be inevitable, but scenario-plan relentlessly, and always have a Plan B (and C, and D...). Coming up with a range of options is often easier when you're objectively planning from a vantage point a few metres back from the cliff edge than when you're already tumbling down it.

- Remember the words of the ancient Greek philosopher Epicurus: 'No evil lasts forever nor indeed for very long.' This too will soon be no more than a memory, and even the memory will fade. Hold on in there.

8. Communicate (x3)

In the context of house buying, we're all well aware by now that our order of priorities must be (i) location; (ii) location; and (iii) location. When it comes to crossing the road (an activity in which my children possess terrifyingly little natural ability), (i) stop, (ii) look, and (iii) listen has been drummed into (most of) our heads. But what of getting through the eye of the storm in a crisis, with sanity maintained and at least a modicum of success? What then should our mantra be? A clear and easy answer:

1. Communicate
2. Communicate
3. Communicate.

I returned to work when my first daughter, Mathilda, turned

one. Tina, an earnest Polish girl keen to live in England so as to improve her English, moved in with us, and leant a hand with the nursery run and with some cooking and housework. Tina adored Mathilda and also, so it seemed, loved to clean. She had never been an au pair before, and I had never had an au pair before, so for both of us, the relationship began fairly cautiously. It felt strange having somebody living with me who was like a house guest, but an employee at the same time, and who was welcome to spend time with us, but upon whose privacy and free time I was anxious not to encroach. She didn't have many friends in the area, and her English wasn't fluent, so I clumsily played the role of friend, employer, surrogate family, landlady and language coach simultaneously. In a painfully British way, I'd hint at what I'd like her to do to help around the house, and hope that despite our mutual inexperience and the obvious language barrier, she would brilliantly intuit my intentions.

I asked Tina whether, during the hours that Mathilda was at nursery, she wouldn't mind a little light cleaning and tidying: about an hour each day. Tina hated to sit still, so she took this suggestion and ran with it. I have never seen a person clean so much. Every skirting board was polished, every cupboard front buffed inside and out on a weekly basis. The house shone, but I began to get concerned that Tina was not entirely well. No matter how many times I queried whether she mightn't like to try out a language class or meet up with friends, she'd reply that she still had cleaning to do.

A few months into the relationship, Tina came to me and said that she loved being with us, and adored Mattie, but that she'd found another job, as she simply couldn't manage all of the cleaning. I was baffled. I told her that I'd never been in a house as spotless as ours, and that I had assumed she simply had an obsessive compulsion with cleaning. Tina looked as confused as I did: 'But you told me to clean this much!' And finally the misunderstanding became clear: in our first conversation about our expectations of each other, my request that she clean and tidy for four to five hours per week had apparently sounded a lot like forty-five hours per week...

I have learned. There is never a downside to being absolutely clear in communicating. With some people (and organisations) there can be a tendency to delay news or instructions that we fear are not going to be well received. The equivalent of leaving the disappointing school report in the bottom of our schoolbag for as long as possible, we may look for ways to put off the delivery of bad news, or hide the really awful elements of it amongst the more palatable ones, hoping that the recipient will figure out the extent of the issue for themselves while we slope off anonymously. This is daft. Communicating clearly won't change the nature of the message: it will simply prevent the situation from getting unnecessarily worse as a result of crossed wires or misunderstanding. Once the message has been properly understood, the appropriate action (or inaction) can be taken (or not taken) as a result. And there are few times where excellent communication is more important than in a crisis.

SO WHO WANTS TO KNOW?

I remember being fifteen. I loved school, not cool to admit perhaps, but true. Even then I recognised it as an incredible opportunity to see all of the people I loved to spend time with all day every day, with only the inconvenience of lessons getting in the way of a wholly excellent social occasion. Within minutes of thundering through my front door each afternoon in a race to get a drink and a snack, I'd be lying on my back in the hallway, legs propped up against the wall, and the coil of the telephone wire entwined around my fingers as I talked at insane length with my friends. My dad would walk past and stare with a look of genuine amazement: what on God's earth did I have to talk about for three hours with people with whom I had just spent the whole day, and with whom I would spend most subsequent days for at least the next three years? And my bemusement was similarly real: how could you *not* want to seize every opportunity to dissect the day in minute detail?! The significance of who chose to sit next to whom in double geography? Whether the fit caretaker (a biomedical engineering graduate from Hull) fancied us (he clearly didn't) and whether Louisa's big brother really was best friends with the Hollywood star Jared Leto (nope: total lie). The days simply weren't long enough to fit in all of the chatter with which we were brimming over.

So who was right: my dad or me? We probably both were, bearing in mind our audiences: another verbose teenage girl like me on the one hand, and potentially a similarly exhausted middle-aged man at the end of a long working day on the other. The first step in avoiding the risk of over- or under-communicating is determining who your audience is. In a crisis, it helps to have a checklist to run through of people with whom you may need to communicate, whether to a greater or a lesser degree, as events unfold. Ideally, and I appreciate there are rarely ideals in a crisis situation, you'll have thought this out with the benefit of time and space to consider and pressure-test all of the possibilities, collating a comprehensive checklist of the various roles or functions whose support you'd want to call upon when in a bind. You'll have their contact details ready to hand and their confirmation that their annual training on '*what to do in a crisis*' has been completed.

In the KFC distribution crisis, thankfully, all of the above boxes were ticked. Well, almost all: ironically my online crisis training module was diarised to be completed at the end of the week of our distributor switchover. The cheery reminder pinged into my phone screen to remind me that, in fifteen minutes, I should find my favourite mug, make a brew and take thirty minutes out of the day to refresh my memory on steps to take should I ever have the misfortune to find myself in a crisis. I heard the ping, and I swear I heard Outlook chuckle to itself at the excellent comedic timing, but I was already too deep into conversation with the core crisis team to pay it much attention.

The map of stakeholders, both internal and external, who would need to be included in the communications plan grew organically at a powerful rate.

THE FIRST STAGE IN EFFECTIVE COMMUNICATION

The first stage of communicating is listening. Listening to understand what the true situation is. Listening to understand what questions and concerns are being raised as a result, and which silences should give cause for concern. Listening to pick up on some gems of pure brilliance that are whispered *sotto voce* by people who fear that now is not the time, or theirs is not the place from which proposals ought to be proffered. Yet again, the guidance of a Greek philosopher, Epictetus, rings true: 'We have two ears and one mouth so that we can listen twice as much as we speak.'

With a crisis such as the KFC one, the manifestation of the issue was not in just one place: certainly the bulk of the issue was concentrated at the distribution centre in Rugby, but with over 900 restaurants across the country, there was news coming in constantly with details of orders that were missing or incorrect from day one. Suppliers too were informing us of drivers returning or planning to return to base with their full load still on board, having been unable to get into the depot to deliver their goods. And of course the teams across each corner of the KFC business had detail to impart: the sales levels tapering off across the estate as core stock ran out; the media and PR team picking up the first whispers on social media that customers were getting frustrated at their local restaurants for not having certain items.

The first stories to break were that KFC had 'run out of chicken'. Without the bare essentials such as Original Recipe chicken on the bone, fries, and the packaging to serve them in, the restaurants were not permitted to open. A Kentucky Fried Chicken without these was harmful to the brand image, and customers coming in could potentially be more annoyed at discovering we only had coleslaw and corn cobs available than if we'd simply closed and not raised their hopes and expectations in the first place. Within forty-eight hours of the switchover, more than one in five KFC restaurants in England had had to close. Another twenty-four hours, and half of the estate was shut. With a constant torrent of data coming in from the outset, the message to be delivered out to the restaurant teams and the customers was critical.

The crisis hub therefore quickly became an efficient melting pot where data coming in from countless sources was logged and analysed, and decisions regarding the strategy and necessary actions were taken, then communicated out. Alongside this, additional weighty juggling balls were being hauled up into the air while the team underneath did all that they could to keep them there.

TARGETED COMMUNICATION

In every situation, the range of stakeholders who will need to be kept informed will differ slightly. The relationship with each individual or group will dictate or at least influence the appropriate level and method of communication with each. In the KFC distribution crisis, here's what worked:

Suppliers: the immediate concern was getting goods to restaurants to enable them to trade as soon as possible. From this objective, we worked backwards. Where were the blockers? What or who would be required to remove or resolve each of them?

Early engagement with the numerous suppliers meant that potential solutions could be quickly explored. Where possible, suppliers would deliver directly to the restaurants rather than passing through the depot for aggregation. Other suppliers withheld deliveries, at our request, until the system was healthy again and able to receive them. The relationships between KFC and the suppliers that had developed and been nurtured over the years were instrumental in ensuring that the primary goal for all was to get the restaurants trading: all other details (how should this impact the price? What about the agreed service levels and contractual parameters that should be honoured? How would they need to adapt?) could wait: the downside of delaying now in order to bottom these out vastly outweighed the downside of the slight uncertainty on the arrangements.

Operations and employees: with constant collaboration between the KFC teams (with supply chain, operations and finance doing particularly heavy lifting), the heartbeat of the business continued. Logistics hacks were tested out and folded into the mix: repositioning the stock in the freezers could speed up the picking and packing process; specifying a different method of packing the now reduced range of products onto the wheeled cages could make the job swifter and more efficient for the depot teams. And focusing on what people *could* do rather than on what they *usually* do led to progress and solutions that might otherwise have been impossible, as will be explored later in Chapter 9.

It would be easy to have such focus on the path ahead, and the tasks that remain to be completed, that you forget to bring others with you on the journey. Being affected by a crisis but having no control over how it progresses can be more stressful than having responsibility for ensuring its resolution. For this reason, keep in mind all the people who might be impacted in some way, and with whom you may need to communicate.

Franchisees: as they are the experienced owners and operators of the majority of the UK KFC restaurants, effective communication with them was vital. For most, their businesses were woven so intrinsically into their lives that the ramifications of their restaurants closing could be cataclysmic. Their support would be instrumental in the recovery efforts. Communicating effectively and urgently with over thirty independent business owners is tricky. Uncomfortably for a company that generally operates by consensus, there simply was not time for KFC to follow the usual process of discussion and consultation. Changes that were being discussed and implemented – moving to a standard 'rescue pack' of core items to be supplied to restaurants, for example, instead of trying and failing to meet bespoke orders – were data-driven decisions, which needed rapid implementation if they were going to mitigate the damage as swiftly as possible.

As a matter of routine, the franchisees elect representatives from amongst their number to form a council and represent the community as a whole, particularly in key discussions and negotiations with KFC. The partnership between KFC and the franchise council chairs had never felt stronger and more vital than during the four weeks from 14 February. The two co-chairs of the council, Acky and Andy, could have had no idea when first elected to their positions, many months before the crisis began, of the importance and impact of the role that they would play. Throughout the crisis, both men were invaluable, attending every key meeting with KFC, DHL and QSL, and voicing the filtered content of the thousands upon thousands of messages they received from the franchisee community: 'Should we all hire refrigerated vehicles and storm the depot to grab what supplies we need?' 'Should we buy products from Tesco and use that as a temporary alternative?' No and no again. Without them to reassure their peers that they were included in the inner circle of discussions, and progress *was* being made, that their concerns *were* being heeded, would we have navigated the craters in the road and made it back onto the asphalt as well as we did? Probably not. The little issues would have grown and spread within no time, and focus would have necessarily diverted from crisis navigation strategy to fire fighting.

With the help of Acky and Andy, major updates could be communicated to the wider franchisee community through twice-daily conference calls, and in the regular open forum 'town hall' meetings which were held in the office or, on one occasion, in the British Library in London, to which all franchisees were invited. In this way, the franchise council chairs were able to brief us on the major issues and concerns being raised by the franchisees so that solutions could be discussed and prepared in advance of each open forum, making these events more positive and efficient as a result.

At the town hall sessions, questions could be taken and answered right there in the room. I have certainly looked forward to meetings more than I did those sessions. Held initially in the roof-top office café, on a rare sunny day, I allowed myself to believe that it was the sunshine streaming through the window and heating my shoulders that was causing me to sweat uncomfortably. And yet the meeting finished with hugs and best wishes and thanks on both sides for all that the other was doing to get through this. And each subsequent meeting with the franchise community filled me with gratitude for the trust that they placed in us, and inspired me to try harder and harder to continue to deserve it.

My day-to-day relationship with the KFC franchisees had always been very open and honest: there was always plenty of time for chat and debate, whether in the office, over lunch in a KFC restaurant, on a golf course, on a phone call or just about anywhere else in between. Suddenly, I was in no doubt at all that every minute that I had spent building trust, respect and, in many cases, friendships in the years before the crisis, quite apart from being enjoyable and worthwhile in its own right, was very well spent indeed. There was no room for ego, bravado, games or politics now. There was time and space for one thing only: honest conversation focused on the core goal of getting the system fully functional as soon as possible. I cannot speak for the KFC franchisees, but I hope that they saw in the team, and in me, people trying their damnedest to represent them and their businesses the way they'd choose to if they were in the room.

Customers: when a problem results in neither death nor serious ill health, it could always be worse. I do not therefore aim to position the KFC distribution crisis alongside natural disasters or terrorist acts in terms of severity or significance. Yet it mattered a lot, to a lot of people. To a proportion of the public, it might just have been a hilarious news item: a chicken shop running out of chicken! For many customers, though, it was more than that: whatever anyone else might think about the brand or the food, it is adored by millions, and removing the option of going to grab a bucket of chicken as a long-awaited treat, or as a part of their weekly routine, was at best an inconvenience and, at worst, truly upsetting.

It was very important not to lose the faith and goodwill of KFC's customers. They were all impacted by the distribution failure, but could do nothing to truly understand or remedy it. Retaining their trust and loyalty was a vital job. Thus the stage was set for the marketing and communications team to step forwards and play their part.

In the crisis hub in the office, a large meeting room was dedicated to the communications team, comprising people from both KFC and the external agencies. Here, the team monitored what was being said on social media and in the press, and made sure that the message to our customers was clearly and consistently given in an authentic tone. We needed to remain true to the brand, despite the situation.

The first question that we needed to answer was what to say when we were not yet entirely clear about what had gone wrong or when it would be fixed. We could simply share as much as we knew: some of our restaurants would not be able to open as we didn't have fresh chicken supplies making it through to them.

There's often a temptation for companies to rein back and become more closed up or formal in times of crisis, and communicate only in a very limited or very measured fashion with the world at large. For KFC, it would have felt and sounded false. Instead, we agreed that the team would observe a set of basic guidelines:

- don't blame anyone;

- don't make promises that we can't keep;

- don't say anything that is untrue;

- do engage and be authentic.

Using the KFC website, Twitter and Facebook, we announced that 'the chicken crossed the road, just not to our restaurants', and apologised to our customers:

> We've brought a new delivery partner on board, but they've had a couple of teething problems – getting fresh chicken out to 900 restaurants across the country is pretty complex! We won't compromise on quality, so no deliveries has meant some of our restaurants are closed, and others are operating a limited menu, or shortened hours. Shout out to our restaurant teams who are working flat out to get us back up and running again.

And the media circus began! Questions were asked (*Where the heck is the chicken? KFC you had one job... !*) and jokes cracked up and down the country as the story snowballed and news readers commented, papers analysed and people tweeted in their thousands, rushing to jump on board.

Strength of character is perhaps best demonstrated by retaining your integrity and sense of humour when the chips are (very literally) down and the world is laughing at you. The team knew that pointing the finger and blaming anyone or anything was both premature and unnecessary. What mattered was that our customers and our teams were disappointed that we were not able to open for business as usual, and for that we were genuinely sorry.

Were we making light of the situation? Not at all: the simple fact was that it sounded ridiculous, and we were as incredulous as our customers were that it had happened. We were simply being honest about it, and managing to laugh at ourselves at the same time: it was either laugh or cry! We also wanted to be as swift as possible to make it clear that this was in no way the fault of the people working hard in the restaurants. The abuse that many of them suffered at the hands of irate customers was shocking, and yet they came in every day, hopeful that deliveries would arrive, and ready to take the heat if they didn't. Apologising and improvising when open and, when the restaurant needed to remain closed, cleaning and tidying it until the stainless steel gleamed and the stock room looked more ordered than a library; the restaurant teams were unbelievably resilient, and massively appreciated.

We responded swiftly and directly to questions and concerns as they arose, such as the comment: 'It's disgusting that KFC won't be paying its employees!' Agreed – that would be awful, and that's why every team member would continue to receive their regular weekly pay, regardless of whether their restaurant was open or not.

As for the statement: 'This makes no sense – it must be a hoax, as all of the chicken is frozen and stockpiled', the reply was: nope – all of the chicken on the bone comes in fresh every day and is hand-breaded in the restaurants: no deliveries, no fresh chicken on the bone.

The press office worked around the clock, seriously committed to understanding our customers, and enabling them to see and understand us. So as to prevent customers from making wasted journeys, we set up a new page on our website – *Crossed the Road* – to enable anyone to check online whether their local restaurant was open or not. Through this, the team was able to keep customers updated, communicating on a real-time basis.

LOOKING FOR SHARED SOLUTIONS

It seems perhaps obvious to say, but the relationship between KFC, DHL and QSL was enormously important. Granted, as new relationships go, this had had a rockier start than many.

But the three companies had worked well together for many months leading up to the changeover, and the reserves of goodwill and collegiality were needed now if the wreckage was to be successfully salvaged. Finger pointing was unproductive. At the worst of times, when the temptation to succumb to frustration and anger at the situation was greatest, it was important to remember three simple truths:

1. nobody chose for this to happen
2. taking anger and frustration out on the people busting a gut to get the situation fixed would be counterproductive
3. everybody shares the same goal – of wanting the KFC distribution system to work like clockwork.

Large companies have many layers, in this case split across many geographies. A fruitful discussion and agreement with one counterpart at one level, in one place, did not mean that every person within that organisation, at every level and in every location, would (i) know of, (ii) agree with and (iii) follow the letter of any agreement or understanding reached. Taking care to ensure that we not only communicated well amongst ourselves within the KFC and franchise system, but also that our myriad discussions and agreements with our counterparties at DHL and QSL reached every ear that they should was an important but challenging task. To say that communication was constant in no way overstates it: even in the few hours or minutes of sleep each night, inboxes were filling and text messages and WhatsApp messages were accumulating. Going to the bathroom was suddenly a treat: it was the only place where it was possible to cease communicating for a few moments.

If the situation felt exhausting for those in the crisis hub, it was no better for those in the London meeting rooms or the Rugby depot. Nor for the teams in the hundreds of KFC restaurants struggling, and increasingly failing, to stay open. Desperate for news of when their deliveries might arrive, the teams were glued to their phones, where updates would be sent as soon as each truck was loaded and on the road. Would it reach the restaurants before they closed? It didn't matter: the teams took it in turns to take their share of a twenty-four-hour watch in the restaurants: once the doors closed to the public, the teams did what they could to salvage some value from the situation. For some, this meant the most thorough and comprehensive deep clean of every last corner of the building and equipment. Photos proudly posted on the internal social media platform, Yammer, depicted gleaming steel fryers that appeared to have been recently unpacked from the manufacturer, but had in fact been the subject of the devoted attentions of numerous concerned KFC employees. As and when a vehicle arrived, the attitude within the restaurants was incredible: it was as though Father Christmas himself had just pulled off the M1 to be greeted with a jubilant welcome from the excited teams.

No matter what the challenge is, there are always at least two options: first, take in the scale and depth of the challenge, feel massively daunted, then get stuck in fixing it. The second option is not to give up, but to keep holding on until you're ready to choose the first option.

It always seems impossible until it's done.
– Nelson Mandela

RESETTING PRIORITIES

Leaving the depot at 1am one morning, I headed to a local Travelodge with a colleague, Rob, in the hope of getting a room for what remained of the night. I needed to be in London the following morning, so planned to make the most of the seven remaining hours before my meeting by sleeping at the closest available venue before commuting direct from Rugby, rather than tackling the 120-mile drive home there and then. Waiting for the receptionist to arrive, I watched Rob, who had been living in the hotel for a week already, half slumped onto the counter, eyes closed. A member of the UK KFC management team, he had yet to return to his family from the clasp of the depot. Every day, he led and motivated the teams of people arriving, eager to help, and ensured that their enthusiasm translated into measurable progress. Rob worked twenty-hour days in the depot, not wanting to leave before any of the team had also stopped to rest and the new shift had been fully brought up to speed on what they needed to do.

The receptionist arrived and, without even needing to check the computer, told me that the hotel was fully booked. 'We always are,' he explained. 'With all of the depots here, the workers just book on a rolling basis, weeks ahead.' He turned to look at Rob and, nodding at him, said, 'See, you're a worker, aren't you mate?' Drained of colour and energy, Rob nodded without a moment's deliberation. 'Yes mate,' he replied, monotone.

Not wanting to stand between Rob and the few precious hours of sleep available to him for a moment longer, I headed back to my car, and drove the two hours home in subdued silence.

In a time of crisis, the sooner you can let go of any sense of what *should* be happening, and what you might normally expect, the better. Once you've come through it, and landed a little bruised and battered on the other side, there will be time to reassess your situation, and what you choose for your future. This will be explored in Part IV. While you're in the midst of it, be as malleable as possible: be what the situation requires you to be.

GETTING THE BALANCE RIGHT

So was the level of communication pitched perfectly? Did we succeed in making sure that everybody, from the global CEO of Yum! Brands (KFC's American parent company, based in Louisville) to each and every team member in restaurants across the UK, received exactly the right amount of information, right when they needed to receive it? No. There were inevitably a small number of people in a meeting room at any one time, and an exponentially larger number of people who would be impacted by the decisions made within it.

Would it therefore have been right to immediately turn to WhatsApp and email to begin cascading news to all impacted parties at the first hint of a break in the proceedings? For many reasons, no.

Things changed. A lot. And with terrifying speed. During the core forty-eight hours of intense negotiations with the key representatives of the global heads of each of KFC, DHL and QSL, every time somebody left the room to use the bathroom they'd need to be updated on their return: the chess pieces did not rest in the same squares on the board for very long at all. To share the highs and lows of every step with a wider circle would have potentially been more harmful to morale and progress than beneficial.

But did we try our very best to strike the balance just right? Yes. My God, how we tried.

THE IMPORTANCE OF SUPPORTIVE LEADERSHIP

In the second week of the crisis, the snow came. It had toyed with us for several days, threatening a festive dusting, but then changed tack and engulfed the country in a thick white blanket, mocking the valiant efforts to get trucks loaded and onto the roads by rendering many of them impassable. I needed to get to Rugby, but living at the bottom of a hill on a country lane with a rear-wheel drive car, I had no hope.

Wrapped up at home in comfy casuals, cut off from the world, for twenty-four hours I joined meetings and discussions with the team ensconced in Rugby by phone and by Skype. Conference calls served as a passable Plan B, but with many more people – external consultants and advisors and DHL and QSL employees – joining the calls than I'd met, attributing comments to people and parties was near impossible. A message came through from a colleague: if I could get to an open road, a four-wheel-drive taxi would be making its way towards me to take me up to Rugby.

The distribution centre had developed a reputation akin to the Hotel California: people arriving there for a meeting would find themselves stuffed into safety shoes and heavyweight jackets hurriedly scrambled from the Screwfix hardware store across the road, re-basing themselves in Rugby for days or weeks while they supported the recovery efforts in every which way they could. I was heading back up there for a meeting, but, with the added complication of the snow falling thick and fast, I anticipated I mightn't be back too soon. Grabbing a bag, I filled it with clothes that would win me no awards for style or fashion, but would be entirely practical for several days snowed into a distribution depot in Rugby. If setting off on foot through a blizzard felt like madness, crawling along in the cocoon of the car at 20 mph on the motorway felt even more ill-judged. But the car journey felt like a refuge from what would undoubtedly await. Closer to Rugby, the blizzard abated; the snow thinned. With the sun out, the memory of the Narnian winter in Surrey felt like a lie.

The key questions being assessed were: what was the root cause of the distribution failure? Could it be fixed, so that the service that the KFC system had been promised could be realised? And if so, how? And where should the mounting losses lie?

It had been important to ensure from the outset that the KFC parent company in the US was kept well aware of the situation in the UK. A difficult conversation to initiate, perhaps, but it would have been far worse if their first awareness of the crisis had been via a comment on Twitter or in a newspaper article, of which there were many. It might not be the case with all multinational organisations, but, with Yum!, it felt very much like a pool of protective older siblings across the pond, ready to jump in and do whatever they could to support, guide and encourage.

Messages arrived from the global leadership team: 'We're all thinking of you and cheering you on', and 'Let me know if there's anything at all that we can do for you and the team. Even a friendly voice or ear to listen – anything at all we'll do. Take care. You've got this!' As we poured yet another coffee at midnight to eke out the second wind from hours ago just that little bit further, the messages truly helped. And our daily emails and calls back to the global leadership team ensured that there were no sudden leaps in knowledge, with the press or social media leading the charge and leaving them lagging behind. Despite our best efforts, though, a call or an email could only go so far to convey the slightly hysterical *#ChickenCrisis* fever that had enthralled much of the UK, and that had occupied every waking moment of the KFC teams.

And so they came. Organically, each person took the decision to come to support the team in Rugby and to be on hand to see the issues with their own eyes, and to discuss, eyeballing one another across the table, and battle through the issues and the solutions.

The airspace above London thrummed with the incoming flights bearing reinforcements: a tenured supply chain and distribution expert from within the Australian KFC business, the global CEO, CFO and general counsel of the brand, and further leaders from the global KFC and Yum! boards arriving from Louisville Kentucky, Australia and Europe, contributing their own commercial and legal savvy and negotiation skills. As the immediate operational and commercial challenges and the longer term picture were being scrutinised by us all, with each new arrival the freshly assembled Swat Team felt more complete (although the 'Special Weapons And Tactics' deployed were less munitions and military plans, and more Excel spreadsheets, diplomatic negotiations and legal, commercial and operational analysis).

The Swat Team

ANALYSING WHAT WENT WRONG

The decampment of the Swat Team from Rugby to London took place during the second week: the snow that had divided the UK into inside and outside the Narnian wardrobe was threatening to return, plunging the whole of the country back into deepest winter. Despite the Valentine's flowers, clinging on in their vase at home, my children were suffering from seasonal confusion as they pulled on bobbled Christmas jumpers and ski gloves before heading across the fields and up the hill to go sledging. Together with two of my colleagues who had just landed from the US, I took the train from Rugby down to London, and checked into a hotel.

We had a full day of meetings starting early the following morning, with representatives from DHL, so that we could plan and negotiate with our counterparties. We urgently needed to find a workable route forward for the KFC, DHL and QSL businesses, and a sensible resolution to the disruption that had been caused.

I arrived in the hotel, the heavy revolving door standing guard between the lily-scented reception and the snow-covered street outside. The receptionist politely told me that my room would not be available for some time, but the spa still had appointments available. Would I care to have a massage or some other beauty treatment? Oh – how desperately I cared to have that! I'd be so very easy to please: the therapist need not even trouble herself to enter the room – I could lie quite happily on the treatment bed with the room darkened, a warm towel pulled up to my chest, and sleep for as long as the room was available. A lady walked past me, chatting animatedly with a friend. Was she going to my treatment room? Was she going to spend the day talking about anything other than chicken and articulated lorries and cash injections and guarantees? Swallowing my envy, I reassured the receptionist that, if I changed my mind and wanted a treatment, I would simply return and find her. But for now, I would head to the business centre.

If my second home had at one point seemed destined to be the depot, as it was for many of my colleagues, fate had decided that now it would be 'The Board Room' in a central London hotel. If it were a film, we had reached the part where the heinous crime had been committed, the suspects had been assembled, and the undercover agents had closed in: the full extent of the heist was about to be revealed. Our camp had been established: the Swat Team was in situ, and the teams from DHL and QSL were nearby for discussions. The goal: to agree on how to move forwards commercially. Return flights had been booked for many of our group for the end of the week, so the pressure was on to make meaningful progress swiftly.

At risk of stating the obvious, the service being delivered by DHL and QSL to KFC and the franchisees was clearly not in line with the promises made in the written agreements. Attributing blame where appropriate, and recovering for losses incurred, was going to mean the difference between insolvency and continued trading for some of the businesses impacted by the distribution failure. Reaching a swift commercial resolution was therefore imperative. The catastrophic financial impact on the one side, and the terrible reputational damage on the other, meant that a settlement was in the best interests of both parties.

As the discussions progressed, punctuated by deliveries of coffee, food and water, the compendium of documents and agreements that would be necessary to give effect to the parties' intentions grew. Fortunately, and perhaps a little geekily, I love

legal drafting. 'Oh, I love well-organised filing! Totally satis-
fying!' the global CEO confided when I admitted this. And so,
together with the unwavering support of the wider team, we
drafted, debated, negotiated, and drafted some more.

Before he'd travelled to the UK, the global chief legal officer
had admitted that he wasn't sure exactly what he'd bring to
the party, but sitting in the board room, the answer was clear:
he was a knowledgeable, reassuring presence, experienced in
leading through legal and commercial challenges in five continents, and simply by being present, he added value. He supported and challenged my thinking, stepped in if I needed to
step out, was a second pair of eyes on the growing suite of
contracts, and an unfailing source of encouragement. He made
me realise that if somebody brilliant offers to come and support
you in a tricky situation, there's no need to worry about what
they could do: just say yes.

COMMUNICATE WITH AS MUCH HONESTY AS YOU CAN

Early in the third week, Monica, a tall and glamorous member
of the marketing team, walked into the meeting room where
the general manager and I were huddled around a laptop
preparing an update to share with the franchisees later that day.
Mon was holding her own laptop, which had a bold red image
on the screen. 'So,' she said, smiling a little nervously, 'we
wanted to get your thoughts on this... ' Turning the screen
around, she started to explain her thinking, but it was entirely
unnecessary. I took in the image of our iconic bucket, standing empty, with nothing but crumbs of the Original Recipe
coating lying next to it. And where 'KFC' should have been
printed, the letters 'FCK'.

I hadn't slept for more than four hours in twenty-four for the last week. I was about to walk into a meeting room to explain the inexplicable to a room packed with our franchise partners. The press were camped outside both the office and the depot, trying to interrogate employees as they arrived and left, and all I had consumed for the last day and night was coffee and Pepsi Max. Mon's artwork couldn't possibly have summed up the situation any better. There were a number of obvious concerns: what would the Advertising Standards Agency think of it? Would the public be genuinely offended? Would our global colleagues appreciate the somewhat British humour given the context? Yet if ever there was a clear window letting the world look directly into KFC, the teams, the franchisees, the directors: this was it. Fully prepared to take on the consequences as and when they landed (and the consequences would need to form a queue at that point), I made a few small changes, and told Mon it was good to go. The general manager was still laughing: she was already completely sold.

It would be some weeks before regular references to KFC were absent from the national newspapers, and before friends and colleagues around the world stopped emailing and texting to let me know that the crisis was being discussed ad nauseam in their country too. The dialogue between KFC and the public on social media undoubtedly fuelled this, but it also achieved something significant: it humanised the company. It transformed KFC from being seen merely as a soulless corporate and instead allowed the real spirit and character of the company, and the positive force of the many people within, it to be felt and understood.

SURFACING FOR AIR

After existing in a central London hotel with the core negotiating team for four days and nights, I realised that (i) I had not seen daylight without the protective barrier of a window pane for some time, and (ii) I had run out of clean clothes. It was 8.15pm. As some of the team headed down to the hotel restaurant for dinner and an escape from the now too familiar four walls of the board room, I decided instead to make a break for it, and go shopping. The very idea that I could simply walk out of the hotel and do something as ridiculously ordinary as going shopping took hold, and the excitement I felt as I ran (yes, ran) through the front door and into a waiting taxi is hard to put into words. A few minutes later, I was walking down Oxford Street, breathing in the clear, dark night and relishing the almost forgotten experience of being cold. Most of the shops were closing for the night, but the bright store front of M&S beckoned me in with a whispered promise of fresh underwear and some neutral basics.

I had lent my last clean top to our external lawyer, so both she and I were now in need of supplies. Plucking a basket from a stack by the entrance, I chose underwear and toiletries for both of us, and tried hard to select tops that were in the right sizes and which suited both the fifth-day-in-a-row-in-a-board-room-with-the-same-colleagues and the about-to-hold-a-conference-with-over-thirty-franchisees occasions. I struggled. I was sleep-deprived and found it hard to switch from a contract negotiation and drafting mind-set to an outfit selection one. As 9pm approached, the lights began to snap off, with the clear threat that the shop had every intention of closing as soon as the last few stragglers had left. A loudspeaker abruptly reinforced this warning. I raced to the tills.

Hauling my basket onto the counter and tipping the contents out in a heap, I realised that I had forgotten to find a new deodorant for our external lawyer, as requested, so I jogged back to the cosmetics section while the cluster of M&S employees at the counter began to ring up my selection.

'Sorry!' I gasped once I'd made it back with a floral-scented roll-on. 'I've been panic-shopping!'

The lady on the till laughed, and asked how on earth a person could find themselves panic-buying underwear, tops and floral-scented deodorant on a Thursday night. Goodness, how much detail to go into? I'd been in a meeting, I told her, which lasted four days longer than planned, and now I had run out of clothes. By now, she and her colleagues were finding the situation pretty hilarious. Who did I work for to have meetings like this? I was alone on my side of the counter by now, acres of darkened shop floor behind me, and five curious faces opposite, partly wondering what I was talking about, and partly just wanting me to get a move on so that they could close up and go home. KFC, I told them.

Well! The level of detail that this group knew about KFC's current predicament was astonishing. While I'd been hidden away in the stagnating air of a meeting room, allowing the distribution issues to occupy my every conscious (and the occasional unconscious) thought, the world outside had been busy absorbing all of the emerging details and forming their own opinions on the situation. Discussions and negotiations that had once been sensitive and confidential were now fair game.

'Oh, I bet you wish you'd stayed with Bidvest now!' she told me, while two more M&S employees debated the wisdom in using a sole distribution centre in the 'logistics golden triangle' rather than using several spread across the country. With their wishes of luck and strength, and pleas for the KFC in Addiscombe to reopen soon, I gathered up my bag and stepped back out into Oxford Street. This was the new normal, and the only way was onwards.

KEYS TO GOOD COMMUNICATION

- Map out a crisis communication plan in advance, with a checklist of people with whom you may need to communicate – whether to ask for help, or to keep updated as events unfold. It might be wise to give them advance warning of the role that you're expecting or hoping that they'll fulfil to ensure that they fully understand and agree to it.

- Make sure that you bring your crisis tribe along with you on the journey, allowing plenty of time for debate and questions wherever possible. It's much easier – for them and for you – to give and to process regular updates than to go from 0 to 100 in an emergency later on.

- Listen. Listen with an open mind both to what is said, and what is not said. Listen to who speaks and who stays silent. The silences can sometimes tell a more insightful story than the words.

- Take time to understand how others might be impacted, whether practically or emotionally, by a situation. If you decide not to communicate, consider what that means to another person. If we had failed to take just a couple of minutes to let a restaurant know that it would not be getting a delivery that night, somebody would have spent eight hours in a sleeping bag in the restaurant. Guard your reserves of goodwill: you never know when you might need them.

- Think carefully before engaging in negative

communications: what is the purpose, and what is the likely outcome? Taking anger and frustrations out on the people busting a gut to do something positive might be entirely counterproductive.

- Don't assume that a message has been received and understood unless you personally witness the recipient receiving and comprehending it.

- Be as open, honest and authentic as you can be. If you don't yet know the answer to something, that *is* your current answer. There is a time for joking, and a time for sobriety. There is a time for gratitude, and a time for apologies. Try to recognise the situation and get it right.

- Think about the format that will best suit the audience: if they're going to need to cascade it, a written brief or follow-up memo will make their lives easier and ensure that the detail and accuracy of the message remains.

- Strip away ego, bravado, games and politics: if the goal is to get X fixed, focus every nerve and sinew on that. And don't take yourself too seriously: sometimes your weaknesses will become fair game, and your secrets may be the topic du jour. You *will* survive this: commentary and laughter are not fatal, so don't treat them as such. Worse things happen at sea.

9. Recognise The Canoes

A God-fearing man was at home during a terrible storm. He began to pray as the rain fell and the floodwaters rose. As the water level passed the upper floor of his house, he clambered out of the window and onto the roof, where he continued to pray for salvation. Before too long, a neighbour fleeing his own house came by in a canoe and called, 'Jump in! There is room here for you. We can paddle to safety.' The man shook his head: 'No thank you,' he replied. 'I am praying to God, and I have faith that He will save me.'

As the waters continued to rise, a police rescue boat arrived, followed by a helicopter. Both repeated their pleas to the man, to accept their help and escape the torrents of filthy floodwater. Each time the man refused: 'No, thank you. I'm praying to God, and I have faith that He will save me.' Reluctantly, the rescuers left without him, leaving the man praying as the flood engulfed his home and, eventually, took his life.

He arrived in heaven and requested an audience with God, to demand why, despite his faith and his prayers, he had been abandoned.

'Well!' God replied. 'I sent you a canoe, a boat and a helicopter. All you had to do was get in!'

CHALLENGE THE PERCEPTION OF YOUR LIMITATIONS

It's easy to see what we expect to see. It feels easier and safer sometimes to set our expectations at the level of what we know to be comfortably within reach, rather than open our minds to what might be achievable. In Part I, I suggested that we truly never know what we are capable of until we take the risk of trying. The same applies to our expectations of and belief in others.

One of my children recently asked whether she could help out in the kitchen, and I thought, perhaps uncharitably, that it would be a lot easier and quicker to simply get the job done myself. A burden for me, and a complete fun-bypass for her. Not long afterwards, I was enjoying a lazy Sunday morning lie in. Softly, my bedroom door opened, and my eldest daughter came in. She had baked shortbread, prepared a fruit salad and a cup of coffee, and carefully carried them upstairs on a tray for me to enjoy in bed. Certainly, she had a little help with the oven, but it was her idea and she took the lead and was hugely proud of herself as a result. I simply had not realised what she was capable of, and I hadn't given her the opportunity to demonstrate it, either to me or, more importantly, to herself.

One of the things that I find slightly ridiculous in advertisements for jobs is the often long descriptions of the areas in which the successful applicant will have extensive experience. If the goal of the employer is to employ a person capable of performing each of those tasks or fulfilling each of those roles brilliantly, such an objective will not necessarily be fulfilled by seeking a person who has done them before. The bright and ambitious junior lawyer who has practised only in competition law but is keen to work in intellectual property: how short-sighted it would be to assume that what she has always done is all she can ever do. How much better it would be to welcome talented applicants who are passionate about entering into a new area, even if it means that they have to work like crazy and put heart and soul into getting up to speed. The combination of common sense, enthusiasm, grit and determination is a powerful one. Of course, a brilliant mind will always help in the mix, but many a person has had a wonderfully fulfilling life and untold successes without winning any academic awards. The real success lies in spotting the glowing embers of untapped ability or potential in somebody, and carefully tending them and coaxing them into a powerful flame.

WELCOME ALL HANDS ON DECK

One Sunday evening in the early days of the KFC crisis, I sat with my seven-year-old, trying to explain what was happening and why it meant that I needed to spend the weekend in the office rather than jumping on the trampoline or sitting in front of the fire playing UNO with her. 'So there is chicken, but it's all in a big traffic jam at the depot?' she asked me. Essentially, yes. 'And all of the cooks in the restaurants are upset and worried, because they don't have any chicken to cook?' Yes, I told her; that's exactly the problem. She thought about it for a bit. 'Well, if they can't get on with cooking chicken, why don't they go to the depot, and help the people there to clear the traffic jam of chicken? Then they can all work together to pack it up and send it off to the restaurants.' As it happened, just hours earlier, Jossie's plan had already been put into action.

The colossal Rugby warehouse was almost entirely gridlocked with stock. With more deliveries arriving every hour, there seemed to be no opportunity to clear the backlog, catch up with the now reduced flow of goods in, and the stagnated trickle of goods out. Every hour, the issue worsened.

It looked almost overwhelmingly awful. Across the UK, hundreds of cooks, team leaders, restaurant managers, area coaches and operations directors were growing more frustrated by the hour that, without fresh stock arriving, their restaurants were running dry and closing, and there was almost nothing that they could do. Almost. From franchise- and company-owned restaurants across the country, and from the KFC head office, forty-five of the best and most experienced operators, and the most practical and resourceful minds, headed to the Rugby depot.

It wasn't difficult to find the depot, with the queue of trucks outside, and the frenzy of journalists waiting just beyond the security barrier, trying to get insights into what the issue was behind the closed doors. This newly assembled tribe took in the situation and, together, created processes and systems where others had failed. An HR leader was appointed to help equip the teams with the tools and clothes they needed to work safely and efficiently in all areas of the depot, from the office to the truck yard and the −18°C freezer. The tribe was organised into shifts to work with the existing teams on site to move and unpack thousands of cases through the night (and the next day, and the next night).

Slowly but surely, the warehouse once again became workable. In the space of two days, 20,000 square feet of concrete flooring reappeared from beneath the abandoned pallets and cages that had once stood there. All of the stock was finally stored where it should be; all waste was removed from the warehouse. Teams newly hired to support the KFC business suddenly had experienced partners working alongside them, sharing the burden and dissipating the fear of failure. The differentiation between the teams from DHL, QSL and KFC was gone: instead, there was one team, hell bent on getting the huge, impressive new distribution centre humming the way thousands of people needed it to.

In the KFC head office, too, everybody was challenging themselves to think about what they could do to help, rather than what their day job generally required of them. Having a direct line through to the real-life equivalent of the Justice League (arguably the best superhero team of all time) to leap in, right wrongs, defeat the baddies and generally get life back on track again would have been wonderful; however, superheroes can be hard to reach, so we turned to our existing tribe. Chris, the development director, challenged himself and his team to come up with ways that they could all help. Experts in the process of identifying potential sites for new restaurants, and getting innovative new concepts designed, built and ready to open, the construction and development team quickly realised that their skills could indeed be put to good use now.

One of the emerging issues was that the huge, 50-foot trucks were simply taking too long to go to each of the restaurants on their routes. By the time they returned to the depot, the backlog of stock awaiting them was already mounting up, and the schedules of planned deliveries was slipping many hours behind, leaving some restaurants without stock for yet another day. The supply of trucks equipped to take chilled, frozen and ambient products in the format necessary to meet KFC's needs was finite.

What if, Chris suggested, the trucks could instead be dispatched to a cross-stock, where smaller sprinter vans, or 'radials', would be waiting to take the load and deliver it on to the restaurants? This would enable each truck to return more swiftly to the depot to be loaded and dispatched to another cross-stock. The supply of the smaller radials was much easier to come by. All we needed was the cross-stocks! Within twenty-four hours of challenging his team to find land of X square metres, with hardstanding of Y square metres and a food storage warehouse that met KFC's strict criteria, contracts had been exchanged for the short-term lease of two such premises, with offers on the table for a further four.

With every favour called in and every potentially helpful contact contacted, the challenge was met. A long-standing shop-fitter for KFC offered up a new warehouse that he had had built, but not yet occupied, and said that it would be available for KFC to use for as long as it was needed. And the tribe of real estate lawyers dropped everything droppable and drew up the agreements that were needed to effect the hurriedly struck deals, so as to hit the right note without necessitating months of legal wrangling. We simply didn't have that long.

A new colleague was being interviewed for a role at KFC during the heady few weeks of crisis. Perhaps surprisingly, she said that one of the things that struck her was how very friendly, energetic and positive everybody was (at a time when most were feeling exhausted, stressed and anxious). And she also said that it was utterly impossible to guess what anybody's job title was: everybody was doing so much more, and so many different things than were usually expected of them. Members of the IT team built programmes to track vehicles where the original service promised to us had failed, and worked with members of the ops, facilities and HR teams to keep the restaurants up to speed with details of deliveries that would be heading their way. The European CEO offered to take on the drive to Rugby so that I, riding shotgun in his car on yet another trip up to the depot, could seize a precious couple of hours of sleep after several days without any. I fell asleep to the sound of his favourite playlist and his Scottish lilt on phone calls to colleagues as we headed north once again.

Everybody who didn't have their heads buried in the crisis picked up the slack for those who did, some doing the work of four people to make sure that no balls were dropped, and the plates kept on spinning.

WELCOME IDEAS AND CHALLENGE

One of the very best things about taking the dog on a long walk is the time that I can spend lost in my own thoughts, thinking through challenges that have me stumped, pushing myself to understand better why the uneasy feeling in my stomach is still lingering, and what I ought to do if I'm going to make it disappear. The dog is wonderful counsel: he generally agrees with everything I'm thinking, unless he sees a rabbit, in which case he disappears into the undergrowth for a few moments in an invariably futile attempt to engage the rabbit in play, leaving me to figure things out on my own for a while. When a long and hilly dog walk doesn't leave me with the answers to the questions that I'm battling with, I'll seek out my human tribe to help me.

When I left school, I took a gap year before starting university, and moved to China to teach English to secondary school children in the southern province of Zhejiang. I was going out with a wonderful guy at the time, but the distance between China and England, in an age that fell just on the wrong side of easy access to email and mobile phones, meant that the relationship was challenging. Entirely distracted by exploring China and throwing myself headfirst into myriad new experiences, I was unsure whether to end the relationship, or to try to sustain it. Walking into my classroom one morning, I explained to the class the English language assignment that they would be undertaking that day: 'Imagine you work in the editorial team on a girls' magazine. You have received a letter from a reader who is facing a dilemma with her relationship... What advice would you give her?' That evening, I sat in bed reading the thoughtful words of advice and wisdom from forty Chinese boys and girls, and could finally see what I needed to do.

There's never a downside in seeking and listening to many different opinions and words of advice and wisdom. Some might have no relevance immediately, but might linger in the darker recesses of your mind until they're needed, when they can be unpacked, dusted down, and revisited in a slightly different set of circumstances.

The people whose opinions and advice I seek out most frequently are the people with whom I tend to disagree the most. Why? Because they clearly see situations through a very different lens to mine, and they're more likely to spot something I've missed, or to point out the weak spot in my thinking, than someone with whom I'm entirely aligned. With my most valued colleagues, we regularly go for long walks to discuss and debate, disagree and sometimes argue before getting to a point of understanding, where we can happily agree, or equally happily agree to disagree. Agreeing with somebody is not a prerequisite to respecting, liking or getting along with each other.

If it's valuable to have people in your tribe who will share their views with you, it's even more valuable to have people who are comfortable to challenge you. Michael Jackson was without doubt an incredibly talented performer. He has left behind an indelible mark on the world and an awesome legacy as one of the most successful recording artists in history. During his life, however, I can't help thinking that he lacked friends who were able to call him out and help him to see that some of his ideas were, frankly, bonkers. The conversation should perhaps have gone:

Hey Mike, about the new baby: Blanket is really not a name for a kid. It's more for bedding, you know?

Really? What about Sheepskin-Rug as a double-barrelled name to make it a bit fancy?

No, mate. Still more for soft furnishings. Jim would work, though. That's a fair name for a boy. Also, I'm no expert, but when you hold him, support the head when he's little and his neck muscles aren't developed. And that balcony stunt you pulled with Prince Michael II, you definitely don't want to try that s*** again.

I can't profess to have been a confidante of Michael Jackson, but I'd lay money on the fact that there wasn't a queue of people ready to challenge him, risking the friendship in order to take their best shot at helping him to see what was patently obvious to the rest of the world, but perhaps not so clear from where he stood.

DON'T TAKE IT PERSONALLY,
BUT DO SPEAK UP

In many instances, challenging an idea or a proposition is nothing to be taken personally. I struggled with this for some time: if I had put time and effort into a proposal in which I fully believed, whether plans for a weekend away with friends, or a work strategy for the business to adopt, my sense of satisfaction in a job well done would come not from the offering up of the idea, but from the acceptance of it by the group. Yet this was ridiculous for several reasons. The element that was within my control – coming up with good, workable ideas – should have been my true goal, if what I wanted to do was to add value to the group and offer up a viable option. The element which fell beyond my control – whether or not the group chose to run with my plan – should really not have concerned me.

Certainly, if I believed that, notwithstanding my advice, a truly awful decision was about to be taken, I'd have done my best to make sure everyone was fully aware of what they were about to sign up to, but if the ultimate decision was not mine to make, it would be futile to overly invest in the making of it. Is it arrogance (*I'm obviously right, so everyone should see that and agree!*) or a lack of confidence (*I'm not sure at all whether I'm right or not, but people agreeing with me would reassure me and give me validation*)? Does it even matter? People often disagree with or reject the 'right' way forwards, and others blindly or intentionally follow the wrong way. Such is human nature. And no matter how much we might believe that we know what we're doing, until we stand in the shoes of every other stakeholder and view the situation through their eyes, we'll never have the truly holistic picture.

Imagine you've been invited to a party, and the host has asked that you bring a bowl of rice, and some iced cupcakes to add to the mix. You prepare both. Taking the freshly cooked rice, you tip it into the big serving dish that sits on the table, and stir it in with the other rice already there. You've spent some time icing the cupcakes to the best of your abilities, and now place each one carefully on the tiered cake stand next to a number of others that have been beautifully decorated and delicately arranged for all of the guests to enjoy. The host invites everybody to come and help themselves to lunch. Salad is heaped onto plates, alongside fish and bread, and spoonful by spoonful, rice. Some hands reach for the cupcakes – selecting the prettiest or the most intricate to enjoy.

As you watch everybody happily enjoying the food, you barely think at all about whether they're enjoying the rice that you'd contributed: it's so completely intermixed with all of the other contributions that nobody would be able to tell whether it was yours or somebody else's on their plates. You keep glancing back at the cakes, though: as the best ones go, you feel more and more embarrassed to see that yours still remain. 'Are there any others?' a child asks. No, just these ones left. The child leaves, taking an apple from the fruit bowl instead. 'Who made these ones?' the hostess asks. Was that a slightly disapproving look?

Offer up your contributions and ideas like rice, not like iced cupcakes: once given, the burden of ownership and authorship is severed, and it is simply the property of the group or the decision maker to do with as they choose. If it's lauded and appreciated, great, but the real win is that it positively enriches the group understanding and decision-making. And if it's rejected? It's not yours anymore: you've offered it up already, so you need have no pride of authorship. Success is not about having your proposal accepted, but simply in having all of the options laid out, so that the right decision can be made based on a genuine understanding of the facts. If you've contributed to that in some way, you've already been successful.

PROTECT YOUR PRIORITIES

In the midst of a crisis, it can be easy to develop tunnel vision, and see only the obstacles in your direct line of sight. *What is preventing me from getting to X? How can I resolve it, or how can the journey be broken up into manageable steps?* Yet in the periphery are numerous other factors: people who need support and attention; issues requiring resolution or potential disasters that must be averted if you're to stand any chance of preventing a bad situation from getting a whole lot worse.

Deep listening

Listen to those who are shouting for help – and listen more keenly to those who are staying silent. Fear, denial and disbelief can all prevent a cry for help from those who most need it.

During the KFC distribution crisis, the road to recovery was peppered with red flags and signposts that additional support was needed. The ripple effect of just one person or one entity struggling and failing was important to foresee accurately. The restaurants were closing in increasing numbers, and with little or no cash coming in through food sales, it wouldn't be long before managing cash flow would start to be a challenge for many of the franchisees. If they were not able to pay their debts as they fell due, the suppliers would likely remain unpaid, which, for some, would be enough to destabilise them pretty rapidly. Others would seek to safeguard their position by demanding that the franchisees pay in advance for deliveries, which would have been understandable but futile, given the franchisees had no cash coming in with which to do so. Which came first: the chicken or the egg? It was beginning to look like neither would come at all.

At risk of stating the obvious (or mentioning the piranhas), the first step towards responding to every need in order of priority is taking the time to consider and identify the full range of needs that there might be. You can then dig deeper into each one, see how several might be connected, and how your response should be tailored accordingly. Using the KFC example, the exercise looked like this:

PRIORITY MAPPING

COLLEAGUES

EXHAUSTION, STRESS, PANIC
- ↳ MENTAL HEALTH
- ↳ LOSS OF FAITH IN COMPANY
- ↳ WALK OUTS

COMMUNICATE

QUESTION EVERYTHING

HAVE A PLAN BUT BE PREPARED TO DEVIATE FROM IT

FOCUS ON THE PEOPLE WHO ARE FOCUSSING ON THE CRISIS
↓
REASSURANCE & LEADERSHIP
↓
ROTATE ROLES
↓
REST!!

CUSTOMERS

LOSS OF FAITH IN THE BRAND
- ↳ UPSET & INCONVENIENCE
↓
EXPLAIN WHAT'S HAPPENING
(AND WHERE TO FIND CHICKEN!)

YOURSELF

EXHAUSTION, STRESS
- ↳ COLLAPSE
- ↳ IMPACT ON FAMILY

COMMUNICATE HONESTLY

SLEEP
↓
LET YOUR TRIBE SUPPORT YOU

EXERCISE
REMIND YOURSELF YOU'RE ONLY HUMAN !!

Retain trust, hope & belief.

SUPPLIERS
WITHDRAWAL OF SUPPLY
↳ MASSIVE PRODUCT WASTE
↳ COLLAPSE OF BUSINESS

COMMUNICATE CLEARLY

GUARANTEE PAYMENTS
↓
ALLEVIATE CONGESTION & PRESSURE AT THE DEPOT
↓
SUSPEND DELIVERIES
↓
DELIVER CORE PRODUCTS DIRECT TO KFC

DISTRIBUTION
BUSINESS FAILURE
↳ DOMINO EFFECT ON OTHER BUSINESSES (e.g. KFCs ACROSS EUROPE)

COMMUNICATE ACTIVELY

DIG DEEP: UNDERSTAND THE RISKS
↓
PLAN A, AND B, AND C...
↓
COMMUNICATE AT EVERY LEVEL FROM DEPOT TO BOARD ROOM

FRANCHISEES
BUSINESS FAILURE
↳ JOB LOSSES
↳ PERSONAL DISASTER

COMMUNICATE REGULARLY

PARTNER CLOSELY WITH REPRESENTATIVES
↓
SHARE INSIGHTS
↓
OFFER INTERIM FINANCIAL SUPPORT

COMMUNICATION =

(LISTENING)
SPEAKING

155

We focused on multiple steps simultaneously, with the unwavering belief that the business *would* recover before too long. If cash flow was an issue now for franchisees, loans could be put in place to tide them over with guarantees given to the banks by KFC. And if nervousness about payment was concerning suppliers, reassurances would be given by KFC that no deliveries would be made without the guarantee of payment following. The plates balanced high on turning rods continued to spin.

Employees in the restaurants were also growing increasingly concerned: their restaurant hadn't opened today, and was unlikely to be ready for trade tomorrow given there weren't even rumours of a truck headed their way. Would they be needed to perform their shifts? And if not, if the shifts were pulled, how would their rent or mortgages be paid that month? Should they search urgently for a new job to fill the gap, or blindly hope that the hiatus would be very temporary? Again, we reassured them that they would be paid as normal, and that the ripples of the crisis would not be permitted to spill into every sphere of life until all were engulfed.

But the biggest personal priorities, when all of the hype and the chicken and the finances are stripped away: where were our families in all of this? My little girls set off to go sledging one Tuesday morning, while I worked from home taking phone calls and working at the dining-room table. And when they returned, pink-cheeked, long hair flying, high on the excitement of a weekday spent hurtling down the snow-topped hill, with the dog chasing and barking at the contagious euphoria, they found I'd gone. I'd hiked up to the main road with my case, their daddy told them, where a determined driver had made it through to collect me and head north to the distribution centre. When would I be back? He wasn't sure.

Worse things happen, I told myself; an unplanned absence

of a day or two, or just one week was bearable, and without a doubt, millions faced worse hardships than this each day. But these were my little girls, and without the perspective of the bigger picture, and how many blessings they had available to them to count, they only knew that they missed me. 'Jossie was very tearful today Mrs Nelson Smith,' the teachers told me, 'so she knows just to come for a cuddle whenever she's missing you and feeling sad.' I felt so grateful for the love being extended to my family and to me, whether through thoughtful emails or impromptu hugs or perfectly timed cups of tea, but what I'd have given for a hug with my girls that week! In an imperfect situation, hoping for perfection is pointless, but maintaining a semblance of normality mattered, and chatting through Alexa or FaceTime over breakfast each morning, whether or not I'd made it to bed the night before, helped enormously. And promising a surprise for every day I was away – a tiny rubber duck from the hotel bathroom, or a mini pot of honey scurried away from breakfast, a promise of a hike to our favourite café for brunch and an evening together at the cinema once all of this was behind us – helped to reframe the change as an adventure rather than a hardship.

As meetings in the hotel board room took place with the team assembled from the USA, the UK and Australia, everything would stop as a bedtime in some part of the world rolled around, and freshly bathed little faces would appear on FaceTime for a goodnight chat with Mummy or Daddy in the room.

One evening, we took a coffee break and I slipped into a room along the corridor to speak with my girls.

'What are you all doing at the moment?' they asked. 'Who's there?'

So I took them in. 'Here!' I explained. 'This is the room that Mummy's been working in, and here are my friends.' Paula and

Rog, still sitting at the board room table, waved enthusiastically at the screen.

'Who's this?' Rog asked, taking my phone. 'What's your name?'

And so Mattie and Jossie sat in their pyjamas discussing their favourite food ('KFC of course!' from Mattie) and ages ('I've got a daughter. She was seven once too,' from Rog) with the global CEO of KFC, as he sat in a snowy board room in central London, surrounded by used coffee cups and exhausted colleagues and mountains to climb, but not until after bedtime.

KEYS TO GETTING THROUGH A CRISIS

- **Recognise the canoes.** It isn't always easy to recognise help when it presents itself. Sometimes, the hurtful comments offered by seemingly harsh critics are the very insights that could help you twice as much as any compliment could. And sometimes the unlikeliest of people can be the hidden heroes.

- **Challenge the perception of what people are capable of:** assess them on what they might be able to do, not what they've previously done.

- If you have offers of support from brilliant people, think hard before ever saying no. It's better to have a massively over-qualified colleague by your side, helping to proof-read and make the tea if they're not immediately needed, than to desperately need specialist or technical support and find that you have already declined all offers of help. There is never a downside in having great people around you.

- Never stop scanning the horizon looking for what

might be on its way. The next big success or small breakthrough? The next colossal disaster or road bump? It doesn't matter: keep scanning!

- Take time on your own to think through your goals and ideas, and take time with people who will help you to look through a different lens. Be generous in giving and humble in receiving advice and feedback. Listen to advice, even if you don't follow it.

- Challenge and invite challenge: of your own ideas, the status quo, anything and everything. Be nervous if people always agree with you. In many instances, challenging an idea or a proposition is nothing to be taken personally. Offer up your contributions and ideas like rice, not cupcakes.

- Understand what and who needs to be protected, and protect them at all costs. Others won't make you or your family a priority: it's an important job, but it's for you to do.

- We judge ourselves by our intentions and others by their actions: don't be too hard on others. They might be doing their best too.

10. Recognise That You Are Human

What you are going through may be awful. However, one of two things is inevitably true:

1. This is not a matter of life and death. You will survive it; *or*
2. This is a matter of life and death. You (or someone else) may not survive it.

This is an even more binary summary of the options considered in Chapter 3 (see page 42). Yet regardless of whether your situation falls into the first or the second category, you should bear one point in mind: in the grand scheme of things, it probably does not matter. Nobody ever has survived life itself, so we will all arrive at the same point eventually. If that sounds callous or belittling of what may be a terrible and destabilising tragedy, it is not intended that way: it is simply a suggestion that battling the inevitable, whether mentally or physically, is a futile exercise.

The Serenity Prayer, referred to in Chapter 1, again rings true: we should have as our goal the serenity to accept the things we cannot change, courage to change the things we can, and wisdom to know the difference. If summoning courage to effect change is difficult for some, having the wisdom to know the difference and the serenity to accept the status quo are for many, including me, the hardest elements.

FALL DOWN, BUT GET BACK UP AGAIN

That moment between sleep and wakefulness, when your conscious thoughts have yet to infiltrate your haze of dreams. When anything seems possible. When your only decision is whether to stretch, prise open your eyes and force yourself into the day, or let the pillow claim you, and keep life at bay for a while longer.

This was an incredibly comfortable bed. The plump pillow smelled fresh and unfamiliar, and the room felt cool beyond my quilted cover. I pulled it tighter, stretched, yawned and reluctantly opened my eyes. Heavy gold brocade curtains were caught back with twisted cords, and the snow falling outside cast a chilly grey light across the room. Beyond the balcony, Hyde Park hid beneath a thick white blanket of snow. The room was beautiful. To curl up in this bed, in this room, and read and drink hot coffee and pity the people having to venture out into the snowstorm: this is what I should do.

Dragging my gaze away from the window, I took in the remainder of the unfamiliar room, trying and failing to identify any sign that I should be in it. The suitcase lying open on the floor held neatly folded men's clothes, a couple of items tumbling over the edge, as though frozen in their escape. Pulling myself up, I sat looking down at the nightstand. An ornate gold and glass lamp. My watch, patiently telling me that it was now nearly 6pm. A half-drunk bottle of mango juice and an open box of Nurofen. My pearl earrings. And a room key tucked neatly into its folded card envelope, with a name hand-written on the front. Mr Roger Eaton: the global CEO of KFC. I closed my eyes and with a sickening lurch, every detail of the day came back to me. It had not been the finest of my career.

Fall seven times. But stand up eight.
  – Japanese proverb

From the outset, we had been sprinting to keep up with the KFC distribution crisis. The initial prognosis was that these were merely teething problems, which would surely be remedied by the weekend. Make that during the weekend. Okay, before the end of the weekend. The thousands of people affected by this situation, those within KFC and the franchise businesses, and others working at the numerous suppliers or with DHL and QSL, threw everything they had at getting it fixed. This was nothing that a lot of bright, determined people with a heck of a lot of grit and precious little sleep couldn't sort out. And for the first few days, we made traction. Alternative systems and processes were created; colossal backlogs of stock were cleared; crisis teams were established and plans were made.

But challenges which, in the context of a small group of people and a restaurant, or even a small group of restaurants, might be capable of remedy within a week, present more of a mountain to be climbed when they stymie the operation of over 900 restaurants, and the day-to-day work life of more than 40,000 employees. Giving up and walking away, declaring that this was too much of a behemoth to successfully fix, was not an option: it was impossible to conceive of the KFC brand in the UK failing, no matter what obstacles it encountered. It was too entwined in the social fabric of the UK, and it was the bedrock upon which so many people's livelihoods were founded. With the support of the wider KFC and Yum! team, and the reliance of the franchisees and employees around the UK weighing heavily on the shoulders of the Swat Team, there was no option: the problems simply had to be resolved. Operationally, conceptually, financially, reputationally, contractually, whatever the lens applied, a resolution needed to be found.

More than once, I remember thinking of my girls when they get into a situation with which they are uncomfortable, or that they don't know how to navigate. They'll call a grown-up to help. Playground battles, where the boundaries are being pushed too far, can be resolved by running to the teacher for sanctuary. By week two of the crisis, I would wake each morning (on the occasions that I'd been able to go to bed in the first place) with embers of hope that we could call in the adults, the teachers, to make this situation go away. But before the embers could be coaxed into flames, the swift realisation hit me: we were the adults, the teachers, and this would only be fixed if we fixed it. The burden of that responsibility can sit like a stone in your chest, growing heavier each day as sleep deprivation gets more acute, and the appreciation of the treacherous road ahead, and of the people who are relying on you to safeguard their best interests, only deepens. These are the times when you need to remind yourself that even responsible adults are only human and sometimes you simply can't go it alone.

A number of meetings took place in a glass-fronted room in the Rugby distribution centre. Representatives of each of the parties debated furiously inside, while wider teams toiled tirelessly outside of the glass, bringing order to the chaos. It is fair to say that the meetings were not fun in the slightest: the subject matter being discussed was depressing, and many of the people present were at or close to breaking point.

When I stepped out at one point to refill a bottle of water, a colleague came up to me looking worried. I immediately smiled at him and started chatting, but he stopped me, and asked, 'Is everything okay?' He'd seen my face during the meeting, he said, and thought I looked completely grey and beaten. 'I've never seen you looking like that before,' he told me, 'and it worried me.' Everyone in the process had their own burden: it was unfair for me to write mine across my face, and worry anybody else who was already dealing heroically with theirs. I assured him that all was well, and I was perhaps just deep in concentration, and I made sure not to let the mask slip in that way again.

As the last day of week two of the crisis merged into the first day of week three, the Swat Team had decamped to the board room of the London hotel. With all of the key decision-makers for KFC in the room, we were intent upon getting a complete solution nailed down within a few short days. The mood was collaborative and positive, but desperately intense. Every contribution was listened to and evaluated, but there was no time for meandering debate. Where, ordinarily, a theoretical idea could be discussed and then explored in more detail offline, with a conclusion settled upon in due course, here, the need for certainty and action was immediate.

I sat at the long board table, and my mind wandered from the meeting to the crazy two weeks that had just passed. The urgent decision-making, the conferences spent standing in front of dozens of concerned and occasionally angry franchisees as they shot questions at me about what was happening to their businesses, and all that journeying back and forth to Rugby... Looking around the room at faces, once so familiar to me, each suddenly seemed distorted and somehow wrong. And their voices: once clear and definite, now blurred into indeterminable sound. I felt utterly confused. I could see mouths moving, heads nodding, but could make no sense of the words floating like helium balloons around the room.

Chris, sitting beside me, nudged my elbow, looking at me

quizzically. 'You okay?' His face was obscured with pricks of bright light, and I couldn't draw out the words needed to reply to him, to say that I wasn't sure that I was okay after all. I felt scared. I was entirely out of my depth. How could I possibly be of any use to the team if I didn't understand anything that they were saying? What if they realised that I was now a dead weight, and asked me politely just to go? Aware that I hadn't been able to utter a word for some minutes, I shifted in my chair uncomfortably, lost my balance, and reached out to the table edge for support. My fingers, gripping it, were numb. So too, I realised, was my nose, which tingled as though I had walked into a hot room after spending too long outside on a frosty night. The voices in the room continued. Confused, I realised that some were directed at me, but I had no idea at all what they were saying as one word flowed continuously into the next and the next and the next, leaving me no time to decipher what each one meant. I felt like I was drowning, my grasp on the present now entirely released as I fell deeper and deeper.

My boss stood at the other end of the table, brow deeply furrowed as he looked at me, his mouth moving and his words merging with the others in the room. In a few short paces he was standing next to my chair, pulling me into a hug, as I burst into tears. I have no recollection of what he said, but I can still feel the enormous relief of finally being thrown a lifeline: *You're not okay, and I can see that, and I can help.*

'Sarah needs to sleep! Is she checked in?' said an American voice.

'No: she came straight here. Where's her bag?'

'Here! I've checked in already. Take my room key. Someone needs to help her upstairs.'

Someone comforting, and help to my feet. More words. More movement. And I was out in the corridor, Paula's arm around me as I walked blindly, crying silently. A lift. A room.

A bed. Paula kindly ordering me to lie down as she fetched a juice and some water from the minibar. And then I was alone, and the room was dark and quiet. And then nothing.

You might think that, after a certain number of things feel completely surreal, you'd simply accept that reality has shifted and everything experienced is, in fact, entirely normal. Lying in the global CEO's bed, recalling being led, crying, out of a room full of some of the company's most senior leaders, is a sobering experience. I had no point of reference on which to anchor this. No similar situation that I could draw upon to remind myself that this was all par for the course, and many before me had done just the same.

Had anyone else ever done this? More to the point, had anyone done this and survived, their career intact? And what next?

Should I stay here and hope that he'd simply find another room, leaving me to emerge, days later, after they'd all left the hotel? Could I possibly front it out and walk back in? There was a dinner planned for that evening with a group of twelve of our franchisees. We needed to discuss the recovery strategy with them, share with them the current position, the challenges and the critical factors that needed to be addressed, and align on the best proposal for navigating a path through the crisis to a solution that could work for all parties. If the franchise community and KFC pulled in different directions, the chasm left between us would threaten to destabilise a number of businesses, and make recovery for some impossible. I was needed there, so how could I possibly spend the evening in bed while the rest of the team went on without me? The absolute fog that had clouded my mind and cut me adrift earlier that afternoon had lifted. Now I was simply embarrassed.

I sat up, swung my legs out of bed, and walked to the window. The room was silent. Hyde Park, a snowy oasis, was scarred by footprints, with new chains being etched into the snow as I watched. 'Come on, Sarah.' I spoke aloud. I straightened the bed cover, and washed my face in the bathroom, trying to figure out what to make of my reflection. 'Come on, Sarah.'

As the bedroom door closed behind me, I retraced my footsteps from a few hours previously. Into the lift. Across to the business centre, and up the stairs. 'Come on, Sarah.' Hand on the door handle. God this was uncomfortable. Just open the door. Now push. Now step in. The room was full – the team still all present. As I stepped in, a chorus of smiles and applause, and a chair pulled out for me. 'Well done Sarah! Welcome back!' And happily, life continued.

THE PRICE OF STRESS

I thought a great deal about sharing these details. It's embarrassing for many of us simply to admit that we are human, and that this inevitably means that we can sometimes be weak and fallible. But we are all weak and fallible at times. And the moment that we are able to acknowledge this and allow others to help is a turning point. Only then will the impossible slowly start to look achievable again. And only then will hope return.

We all have our limits. We don't necessarily know where they are, but as and when we hit them, it becomes clear that whatever the heck Plan A was, it's time to let go of the hope that we'd nurtured, and instead open our hearts and minds to the possibility of a successful outcome with Plan B.

One of the bravest and most inspirational things I have seen recently was a speech given by a member of the campaign led by the Lord Mayor of London's Appeal charity, called 'This is Me'. The campaign has recognised that:

> … as a nation, our mental health is becoming increasingly vulnerable – and workplace stress is a leading cause. We all deal with

stress at work, but for one person in every three, it's so extreme that it becomes unmanageable. Mental health is still shrouded in stigma, and half of all those experiencing a mental health problem don't disclose it to their line manager, fearing reprisal, judgement and discrimination. As a result, people continue to suffer in silence before eventually reaching crisis point. Even more distressing is that this can be prevented.[1]

The campaign, together with a number of partners, seeks to reduce the stigma of mental ill health, particularly in the workplace, and to raise awareness of wellbeing. One of the ways that they do so is by encouraging employees who have experienced mental health problems to share their stories with their colleagues by creating a video message.

On the campaign's website, a number of video messages have been posted by bright, articulate professional people, sharing their stories about their own struggles with mental ill health. As I watched story after story, my admiration for these people grew, as did my realisation that I would really struggle to admit my weaknesses in the way that they had. Rather than admit that I was exhausted and stressed and needed a break, I pushed myself until my body made the decision for me and started shutting down. And even after this breakdown, I still felt embarrassed about what had happened. I could perhaps tell a friend about passing out, but I certainly couldn't mention that I had cried!

But what if that friend had also found himself boxed into a situation with seemingly no escape? Might it have helped him to ask for or to allow help if he realised that he was not alone in struggling sometimes?

When working in law firms in the city, I have seen and experienced horrendous levels of stress and mental ill health. As a trainee, I witnessed a colleague who had not left the office for three days try and fail three times to leave the room to go to the bathroom. Each time, he stood, staggered blindly towards the window, then the book case, before finally asking me whether I could help him to find the bathrooms. I led him there then, not knowing what else to do, went back and carried on with my work.

We all have a breaking point. I had first experienced mine when, as a heavily pregnant lawyer, working twenty-hour days, seven days a week, I fainted in a senior colleague's office. Whether through stress or exhaustion, my body had had enough and while I was sitting discussing the possible ways to bolster the weaknesses in our legal position, I passed out. The first thing I saw as I opened my eyes some moments later, chin slumped to chest, was the swell of my stomach, my first child curled up inside it. The second was the partner, sitting at his desk typing, as though it was entirely normal to have an unconscious pregnant woman slumped in a chair opposite him. Whilst the older, wiser me is fuming, the younger, naïve and heavily pregnant me simply apologised (apologised?!).

'I'm sorry,' I said, refocusing on the room around me, 'I just keep getting dizzy and passing out.'

He didn't look up. 'No problem,' he replied. And kept typing.

And I went back to work.

The absolute failure to recognise and call out the obvious impact of stress on a person's mental health in these and, unfortunately, a terrifying number of similar situations, is not acceptable. Most people would not hesitate to jump in and help or call for help if they witnessed somebody suffering a heart attack, or someone who had fallen and broken a limb. And the victim in each scenario would no doubt welcome the intervention. But a person suffering mental ill health falls into more of a taboo category.

I am under no illusions: I am not an expert on mental health, and I will not insult people who battle with mental health challenges by proposing trite resolutions. I know that a 'quick fix' is unrealistic for many sufferers. But we can continue the conversation, and encourage others to do likewise.[2] We can seek out opportunities to be there for people who might need a strategically timed hug or cup of tea and a chat. And we can share stories of our own times of weakness, to remind ourselves and others that we are human too, and that that's okay.

THIS TOO SHALL PASS

The days rolled into one another. The sprint to get the KFC business thriving again and the distribution system to the level that everyone had so eagerly anticipated turned into a marathon, with new runners arriving each day, new theories and plans being implemented. Brilliantly logical proposals failed, and were quickly replaced with improved possibilities. Ideas were offered up like sacrifices to be challenged, pulled apart and then either followed or discarded.

And the efforts of so many began to pay off. While the world outside KFC continued to turn, with jokes and questions about what had happened, the world within KFC started to catch up. Restaurants re-opened; limited menus expanded; the teams from DHL and QSL got into their rhythm, working together and anticipating obstacles so that they could be moved or avoided rather than slammed into at breakneck speed.

Then, one evening, I went home from work. I stepped through the door before my children had been tucked into their beds, in time to chat with them and hear all about the adventures of their day. I kissed them goodnight with promises to still be there with them in the morning, and went upstairs, with a large glass of Rioja, to run a hot bath. My phone lay silent and ignored on the windowsill, obscured from view by the softly flickering scented candle, while I spent a whole wonderful hour submerged beneath the bubbles, doing nothing more challenging than breathing deeply and topping up the hot water from time to time. Luxuriating in the heat and the silence, and with a growing feeling of hope and relief, it was only then that I realised: we had emerged, exhausted but unscathed, with the most intense period of crisis finally behind us.

Sometimes, it can be hard to identify the exact moment that a period of crisis ends. A failed parachute suddenly opening or flames finally being extinguished are easy to see and to celebrate. As will be considered further in the final part of this book, the end of the crisis may be indicated only by clues and subtle pointers: fear gradually receding, and life slowly feeling manageable and 'normal' once again, even if the new normal is very different to the one you previously knew.

Through perseverance many people win success out of what seemed destined to be certain failure.

– Benjamin Disraeli, British prime minister, politician and writer

KEYS TO BEING KIND TO YOURSELF

- Acknowledge that you are human and that you will be weak at times. And so will everybody else. Having a breaking point is normal, but have faith that there is a fixing point too. Life will go on.

- Look out for friends and colleagues and be there for them if you can. Whatever it was that made my colleague Julian come quietly into the meeting room with a cup of tea for me as I sat, exhausted, on a

conference call in the midst of the crisis, thank you. It
meant a lot.

- Think back to your reflections on understanding how
  to find your comfort zone, and don't be a stranger to it.
  Your most important role is sometimes to take care of
  yourself.

- Find those people who love you enough to be honest
  with you, and listen to them. They may be more
  objective about your strengths and weaknesses than
  you are.

- Care (about success, failure, stuff). But not too much.

- As discussed in Chapter 3, sleep is ridiculously
  important. Lack of sleep can lead to weakened
  cognitive abilities, poor performance, and ill health,
  both mental and physical. Don't underestimate the
  impact it can have on you, and the adverse filter that it
  can cast over your perceptions.

- Giving 100 per cent in every area of your life is
  impossible. Losing it with your kids when you get
  home from work exhausted and ready to snap happens.
  Taking a moment to cool down, before apologising
  and explaining to them what's happening with you is
  surprisingly easy and cathartic, and teaches *them* that
  it's okay to be human too.

Part IV
Recover

Just as you need to be able to recognise when a crisis has begun, so too do you need to be able to recognise when it has passed. At some point, it will cease to be a crisis, either by life returning more or less to normal, or by the current state looking like it's here to stay, in which a 'new normal' has arrived and will need to be embraced. Either way, the period of high octane, high intensity collaboration and response is not sustainable indefinitely. And when it passes, ensure it passes consciously. Follow up on any outstanding actions and any lingering items on your to-do list; return the phone calls you had no time to acknowledge earlier; reconnect with people who were involved along the way, and take the time (now that you have the time) to explain to them what has happened, what is likely to happen next, and what they might be able to expect going forward. The best way to prevent mistakes from being repeated is to ensure that lessons are understood, shared and passed on for the benefit of whoever might pass along the same path in the future. Don't rely solely on the memories of people who may not be there as and when the pattern repeats itself. Make a record of what has happened: time will move on and this too will become little more than a memory. Even the starkest of memories will fade.

11. Learn!

Clearing up and preparing to move on from a crisis can be cathartic. Walking past the KFC crisis nerve centre one morning in March, I saw that the blinds on the door had been lifted. In the meeting room that had been home to the logistics tracking team, a group of restaurant managers sat in a training session debating and laughing. I stood for a few moments watching them, smiling. It felt almost like there had been a death. Dramatic? Perhaps, but the lives of so many people had been wrenched out of their control, as their businesses and livelihoods were laid on the line. Franchisees, KFC, DHL and QSL and all of the people within each of the companies who had endured weeks of uncertainty, intense stress and hour upon countless hour trying to achieve something that seemed at once so simple and yet infuriatingly impossible. The businesses that we'd known before the crisis were gone. Relationships had been tested to their limits.

And what was left behind? The bits that mattered. The insights into what people, individually and collectively, could achieve, whether wearing the same shirt that they'd pulled on forty-eight hours previously, or a hurriedly purchased high-vis jacket and safety shoes. The memory of a person pushed beyond the point of exhaustion into abject defeat, trudging through the depot yard at 2am after a twenty-hour shift, only to paste the game face back on as soon as a colleague was spotted and heartily congratulate him for some new success.

Cleanse the air of crisis

Accept that the situation is what it is: no matter how much you might wish it, you cannot rewrite the past. Nor can you fully understand the impact that it has had on others. Speak with them. Listen to them. Invite people to explain to you how it seemed from their point of view, and how they feel about the situation now. Often people simply want an opportunity to be heard, to feel that they matter, and are appreciated. Listen actively: recognise that your answers and solutions are not necessarily what's needed here. It may simply be your listening ear and your patience that are called for.

Learn the lessons of what worked, and what didn't. Take responsibility for the role that you played in it, and perhaps the role that you should have played, but did not. In business situations, file away plans and documents swiftly constructed, and share with all who would benefit from reading and learning or remembering the content. Cross the t's and dot the i's. There is time for this at last.

Thank the people who gave their all, whether drafted in in haste, or who opened the door themselves in order to step into the eye of the storm simply because they spotted some new opportunity to help and seized it. Cleanse away the air of crisis.

UNDERSTANDING WHAT WENT WRONG

In addition to taking stock and learning from the facts during the crisis, take the time afterwards to analyse what really went wrong. Where mistakes were made, why? If you hope to retain your integrity and credibility, take ownership of your decisions, whether good or bad, of your actions and your inactions alike. Was there a fault with a process or a system or a person? Should there be any significant changes as a result? And if not already achieved earlier on in the process, depending on where the blame lies, what recompense or consequences should there be? Whilst this element might be inevitable and is certainly important, it's just as important not to leap to this step too soon. Let the dust settle before trying to write in it.

What went wrong?

People

- Were the right people involved at the right times?
- Were work and responsibility allocated appropriately?
- How effective and timely was communication?
- Did everyone understand what they needed to do?

Planning

- Was there sufficient risk analysis, mitigation and contingency planning?

- Was there appropriate due diligence into both the solution and the supplier?

- Did the agreement on paper reflect the parties' understanding?

- Were appropriate timelines for key steps and decisions followed?

- Was there a clear implementation plan?

Process and governance

- Did all relevant stakeholders have an opportunity to question and input into the process?

- Were any issues escalated and resolved at the right levels?

- Were all agreed steps followed?

- Were parties held to account for performance and outcomes?

POST MORTEM

Whatever the nature of the crisis, it may be that the people best placed to look dispassionately into the detail and discern from it the key lessons are people new to it, with no existing link to it, whether emotional, financial or practical. This might mean instructing external experts to conduct a thorough post mortem review of what transpired, or simply turning to a friend, counsellor, mediator or colleague to look with a fresh pair of eyes at the same facts that caused such disruption.

Whichever approach is taken, be completely clear about your expectations. Are you looking for analysis into the root cause of the issue so that you can determine for yourself where the best laid (or not...) plans went awry? For blame to be attributed? Or are you looking for a fairy godmother to flit in and make everything all right again, to ensure that lessons are learned, the culpable parties held to account and wrongs righted? If so, you may need to manage your own expectations.

There are some losses that can simply never be recovered. Financial loss may fall into this category if insurance cover is insufficient, if indemnities or warranties don't go quite far enough or if recourse through formal dispute resolution channels is cost-prohibitive or too uncertain to be a commercially sensible choice. But the greater loss is of time: time that you should have been spending at a close friend's engagement party, or time that you should have been spending focused on *Her* or *Him*, when your mind was instead fully occupied with *It*. And the period of stress, of sleepless nights and exhausting days prompting grey hairs (or less hair) and worry lines etched a little deeper than they once were. Accept the limits of what can be rectified. If the impact of the crisis cannot be erased, it should be embraced as another chapter of the story.

The most important lessons are often the hardest learned. By experiencing a crisis, successfully navigating a way through the worst of it and emerging stronger and wiser on the other side (even if you need a period of recovery and reflection before you *feel* stronger and wiser), you've gained something incredibly valuable. There will doubtless be numerous mistakes in life that you've yet to make, and many more losses to suffer, but this is one that is less likely to be repeated. This is one that, by understanding what went wrong, and sharing the lesson with others, will better prepare you and those around you for the future.

This is a wonderful opportunity to make great change, so don't shy away from it. Talk. Be cautious about 'being British' about the whole situation and going down the route of *least said, soonest mended* and *let bygones be bygones*, for example. Don't talk about a negative situation, and it will go away, right, almost as though it never happened? More likely, though, that it will fester in the hearts and minds of those affected, who never had the opportunity to vent, to share their thoughts, their anger, their ideas on how to prevent it from repeating itself; more likely that it will repeat itself.

THE SARAH CURVE: (HOW TO) DEAL WITH IT!

There are many ideas and theories on how people react to and move on from difficult situations. One model with which I cannot help but feel an affinity is the 'SARAH curve'.[1] It acknowledges that change, in any context, can be unsettling, and proposes the five stages that the majority of people will experience to some degree as they respond to, and come to terms with it. By understanding these stages, it's easier to believe that the process is entirely normal, and that it is possible to progress through to embracing the new normality eventually. By recognising the journey that others may be passing through, it is also easier to reach out and help to support them through it.

SHOCK: The initial reaction is one of shock. You might find it difficult or impossible to believe or accept what has just happened, and might cast around for somebody to blame it on.

How can I get through this? Give yourself time to think and to process the facts. If there's more information that you need in order to see the bigger picture, seek it out. Don't try to fix this: simply aim to understand it, as objectively as possible.

How can I help others through this? Listen. It's too soon to rush in with justifications and explanations. At this stage, simply be available to let others know that they are being heard, even if neither of you are able to change what's happening.

ANGER: Once the reality and the implications of the situation are realised and understood, shock can give way to anger. *This should not have happened!* You might move on from blaming others, to being self-critical, and worrying that this is perhaps your own doing. This is a hugely stressful stage.

How can I get through this? Again, try to explore, question and understand rather than blame. It may help to collate notes or details of your understanding, so you can reflect on it dispassionately after taking time to sleep on it and discuss it with members of your tribe. If appropriate, talk it through with somebody who is not also trying to work through this part of the curve.

How can I help others through this? Listen patiently, and discuss with others directly so as to avoid the group hysteria of multiple angry people whipping up the waters even more than might be necessary. If this happens, try to coach and support others through the process, so that the path is laid for them to follow.

RESISTANCE: Denial may set in – the situation is so far from what we hoped for that it cannot be happening. Whilst the idea of accepting the situation, supporting each other and making the best of it is initially met with derision (*I want no involvement* *in this: you're on your own now!*), elements of doubt and perhaps the first glimmers of acceptance might flash through.

How can I get through this? Keep an open mind. People have probably survived worse and lived to tell the tale, or faced disaster without losing all hope. Could there be some good to come of this? Might a silver lining be lurking somewhere beneath the surface? Start piecing things together now: you have the background, or the edges of the jigsaw. Start sifting through the jumble of pieces in the middle and trying to imagine how the completed picture will appear.

How can I help others through this? Collaborate. Share ideas and hopes about how this could come together. Call upon others (expert advisors, experienced colleagues or objective friends) to help to bring the positives and the possibilities into focus, and to allow the anger and resistance to recede.

ACCEPTANCE: It feels like the clouds are beginning to clear. This is when the mind-set shifts from negative and retrospective to shards of positivity and a focus on the future. Discussions no longer revolve around what has been lost, but on what might be gained from the experience. Discussions are exploratory: *If we're going to get through this, perhaps we could try... If this is going to be the new normal, maybe X could make it more palatable...* How can you move on from here? You have come to terms with the change and are ready to accept or live with it. It's now that the benefits of the new normal can be realised.

How can I get through this? Take action. You've discussed, analysed and contemplated. Now is the time to do. And take ownership of your path, both up to this point and leading on from it. Make plans; test out solutions or alternatives. Think to the future, and prepare to step into it.

How can I help others through this? Encourage others to start thinking ahead, and mapping out the role that they (and others) will step into. When you are ready to let go of the anger and retrospection, make sure that you're there to encourage and reassure them.

HEALING/HAPPINESS: Analysis and review have high-lighted the errors of the past, and these have been instrumental in creating new processes, systems and roles; this is, finally, the new normal. The change has been accepted. The crisis has passed. People have learned (or some may still be learning) to adapt to the current situation.

How can I get through this? From your new standpoint, give yourself licence to look back, and, with the benefit of hind-sight, assess the process you've just been through. How has it changed you? How has it changed the way you view your corner of the world, and the people within it? Regardless of whether you chose this or not, and regardless of how much of a toll the journey has taken, some good will have come of it. Embrace it, and look ahead for the next mountain to climb.

How can I help others through this? Be ready to catch others as they teeter on the edge of falling back into resistance or anger. Hold their hand, and help them to focus on what they've learned, and how they've grown.

My head of sixth form, Mrs Casebourne, was a devotee of the 'what doesn't kill you makes you stronger' school of thought. I agree with her wholeheartedly. Just keep trying.

> Holding on to anger is like grasping a hot coal with the intent of throwing it at someone else; you are the one who gets burned.
> – Buddha (attrib.)

BRING ALL THE PIECES TOGETHER

After the KFC crisis, I spent a lot of time speaking with people about it, with others telling me details that I perhaps already knew, but from their point of view. It became their story. Sometimes, I simply listened, and thanked them for all that they'd done. Other times, I sat with them drinking too many cocktails and laughing at the worst moments, which at the time we never imagined we'd be able to laugh about.

With six of my team some months later, we lounged in overstuffed armchairs in an old townhouse in Bath, mugs of hot tea in hand and plenty of biscuits within reach, and spent time asking each other the questions we hadn't previously had the time to explore. Together, we held most of the jigsaw pieces, but individually, we had held only fragments of the picture, along with the knowledge that there was more to come.

We discussed the whole episode at length, explained, challenged, recognised, thanked and, when we had nothing left, we packed away our pens and books, returned the mugs to the shelf, and walked down into the city for an evening of good wine and food, fantastic company and plenty of laughter. There was suddenly so much more to think about than that crisis.

KEYS TO LEARNING FROM YOUR EXPERIENCES

- **Today's unholy nightmare is the wonderful development opportunity that you reflect upon tomorrow. Hold on in there!**

- Accept the limits of what can be rectified. If you cannot change it, accept it. If you cannot accept it, leave. Staying and tormenting yourself with what you wish were the case is self-destructive, and will have a negative impact on those around you.

- Offer people an opportunity to be heard, and to feel that they matter and are appreciated. Focus on listening actively and patiently, rather than on trying to identify and propose solutions.

- Take responsibility for the role that you played, and perhaps for the role that you should have played but did not. If you hope to retain your integrity and credibility, take ownership of your decisions, whether good or bad, actions and inactions alike.

- The emotional journey people, perhaps you, will need to experience in order to process the change or the impact that it has had may feel almost like a second wave of crisis. It is what it is. Do your best to help yourself (or others) through each stage, but appreciate that sometimes you simply have to cling on and wait it out with an open mind.

- Let it go...

12. Know When To Walk Away

If you stand at the foot of a mountain, all you can see is the mountain towering above you intimidatingly. You need to climb to the top of it or get away from it to appreciate that the world is made up of many millions of features, of which the mountain is only one.

*

Never underestimate the strength, power and insight that you can gain simply by walking away and gaining some perspective. You might be absolutely incandescent that somebody has reversed into your car, but if a close friend or family member falls dangerously ill the next day, you'll think longingly back to the time, only hours previously, when your most serious concern was no more than damage to a vehicle. You may be all-consumed by the nightmarish crisis that is unfolding hour upon hour before your eyes, but if you prise yourself away from it, grab the dog and go for a walk, a few things will become immediately obvious:

1. the dog does not care about your crisis: he is simply delighted to spend time with you, overjoyed to be going

186

for a walk, and optimistic that there may well be a tasty treat about your person;

2. the many people you pass are also unlikely to care too much (if at all) about your crisis; and

3. notwithstanding (1) and (2), the world is still turning.

Your crisis need not be anyone else's concern. It may be hard, in the moment, to acknowledge or even believe this, but your crisis needn't be overwhelmingly your concern either. You'll do your best to get safely through it. You'll greedily extract all of the lessons from it that you can, and you'll use them to make positive change and mitigate the risk of such situation (or similar) recurring. But will you let it keep you in its tight and increasingly tedious grasp? Will you let your every conscious thought and every fevered dream, every conversation opener and the focus of every casual chat have as their beginning or their end, the crisis? Perhaps, for a time. But you need not.

Of course it might sound ridiculous to imagine that you could simply step back, take a deep breath and hum 'Hakuna Matata' (the catchy and cheery song from *The Lion King*, based on a Swahili phrase that roughly translates as 'no problems' or 'don't worry, be happy') to yourself as you elect always to look on the bright side of life. The world as you know it might have crumbled, and you may need to decide for yourself whether to throw yourself onto the rubble and allow the sense of loss, defeat and failure to overwhelm you. Or whether to gingerly pick yourself up, and dust yourself down whilst checking for obvious injury. Realising with some relief that actually, you're okay, that you will live to see another day, to fight another round, you may instead decide to chalk this one up to experience. You might acknowledge that you, and those around you, are imperfect, but there's now an imperfection that's a bit less likely to let you get knocked so easily off your feet next time around. Yes, you feel a little older, but wiser too. And, as Sir Winston Churchill famously urged people to do throughout the Second World War as he refused to give in, no matter how bleak the outlook, you keep buggering on.

Retain a sense of perspective

A few years ago, I had just touched down at Gatwick airport after a week away, and a lady and her husband who had been travelling in first class stood opposite me, waiting to disembark. The flight crew were allowing one passenger from the left, then one from the right to pass, so that we all filtered off the plane together.

'Look at that!' the lady remarked, aghast, with a disgusted shake of her head. 'They're not letting us go first!'

Her husband put his hand reassuringly on her shoulder, and soothed, 'I know love; life can be so unfair!'

Get. Some. Perspective.

WHAT REALLY MATTERS

Leaving the office late one Friday night after yet another tough day, I was blocked from leaving the car park by a police cordon. An elderly lady had been walking home from the shops, and a van, reversing at speed, had knocked her to the ground as she crossed the drive. She lay, keening painfully, across the entrance to the underground garage, surrounded by a halo of crushed apples and a split bag of breakfast cereal sprinkled like confetti on the wet asphalt.

I turned off my engine and walked up to the scene. An

ambulance had arrived, and the crew crouched by the lady's side as the police officers took names and contact details from all who had witnessed the accident. As the lady was inched onto a gurney, she sobbed at the indignity of her situation: some of her clothes had been cut from her, and she relied now on strangers to enable her to exit this excruciating tableau.

I stood and I waited. I'd offered my help to the police, and I spoke quietly with the growing group of neighbours trying to enter or leave the building, the hurry that each of us had been succumbing to only minutes previously now gone. My self-pity at leaving the office at an hour when most people were enjoying a big night out was replaced with a quiet gratitude that I was able to drive myself safely home, where my family would be waiting for me.

Having a clear view of the bigger picture of the world outside your own corner of it won't make your troubles disappear. The person who has broken a finger is still in pain, but when they have seen first-hand those who have broken legs or lost their lives, it can make it marginally easier to retain some perspective. Quite aside from the physical or practical hardship that we might encounter, the impact of the emotional reaction to it – *Why me? It's not fair! I feel so disappointed / betrayed* – can be a major blocker to emotional and mental healing. Even if the physical elements are outside your control, you can choose your feelings. If you can take control of them, your problems will be halved.

COMFORT ZONE REFUEL

Having begun this journey together by looking at what is needed to furnish your comfort zone, we have twisted and turned away from that idea, until the very concept of a comfort zone has been almost forgotten. Remember it now. Think again about what it is that you need to feel whole. Remember what it is to have your physical, mental and emotional needs met. The landscape may have changed for you in one or many areas, but your basic need to feel good remains. You may just need a bit of support to get there.

Any crisis can be destabilising, and may go further than simply making you deprioritise your own needs: it can make you forget what they are altogether. Once the eye of the storm has passed, carve out time to spend focusing on yourself: revisit Chapter 2, 'Understanding Your Comfort Zone', and permit yourself to rediscover it. This is not indulgence, although it might feel that way. This is simply checking the oil and water, and topping up the air in the tyres and the petrol in the tank. This is preparing yourself both for the next round of short trips to the shops and to friends, and for the next long cross-country slog: you can never be entirely sure which will be required next.

- *Exercise:* get back into good routines; plan for your next challenge, whether your first 5km race, the start of your marathon training, or simply a regular swim or walk. Re-establish the good habits that were broken, and create new ones where none existed before.

- *Time:* practise not rushing. Spend time in places that are uplifting: hanging out with family and friends; time alone for long walks or bracing bike rides; sitting people-watching on a bench in a packed shopping centre while you nurse a hot chocolate and sit in blissful anonymity. Have a lie-in. Take a long bath. Read the novel. Watch the box set. And if you feel guilt for being so indulgent, remind yourself that this is simply routine maintenance to ensure you're mentally ready for whatever lies in wait around the corner.

- *Sleep:* sleep might have been one of the first jigsaw pieces of your 'normal' life that you hurriedly thrust onto the sacrificial altar in an attempt to appease the monster that was the crisis. Remember those days of waking feeling refreshed and alert and excited for the day to begin after a fantastic night's sleep? If so, rediscover them! Alternatively, if that's a concept with which you have never been familiar, now is the time to discover the restorative power of sleep.

- *Experience:* don't confuse relaxing with stagnating. Resting and growing are not mutually exclusive. Invite new experiences – of your choosing this time – and personal growth back into your life. What have you always (or recently) wanted to be able to do? The new language that you'd always planned to learn. The adventure holiday that you've dreamed of for years. For me, the new experience was sailing: after messing about in boats with my dad as a child, I hadn't returned to sailing since his death over twenty years ago. So I chartered a small yacht for a family holiday, giving myself six months to learn how to sail it and get the necessary certification to be able to do so. Structured learning, coupled with physical challenge in a new arena, felt enormously fulfilling to me.

RE-INVEST IN PEOPLE AND RELATIONSHIPS

When I realised that I was, at last, free to think and talk about something other than the distribution of fresh chicken, I con-sciously and visibly prioritised my family, and said yes to as many things as possible: we took off to Dorset for a few days, and played UNO in our pyjamas for hours, before walking down to our favourite café for a breakfast of cake and coffee. We had a girls' night at the cinema – my children, mother-in-law and I – with an extra-large tub of popcorn or glass of wine apiece, my phone turned off, at home. We held a birthday lunch to celebrate my grandma's ninetieth and my sister's fortieth, and somewhere in amongst the shouts of laughter, tight hugs and wedges of cake, the challenges of the previous weeks faded gently into the background, a healthy equilibrium reasserting itself, as the crisis receded: it was already just another story.

Whilst you've had your head down navigating the crisis, leaning on your tribe to keep you afloat and pull you through it, the balance of your friendship accounts has been quietly depleting. Any friendship is a mix of easy times and tough ones. The hope, of course, is that the halcyon days filled with high spirits and easy laughter outnumber the darker times when worries about health, money, the past or the future weigh heavily on one or other of you. Regardless of the balance, you must make sure that once you have the ability to re-invest in your relationships, you do so. Disconnect from what has occupied you so absolutely in order to reconnect with the people who matter.

In the same way that your friends have had to play second fiddle to your crisis, you can at last allow them to step into centre stage. Instigate the nights out (and evenings in) that you'd pulled the plug on previously, and, when you're with them, make sure that your phone is turned off and you're truly in the moment at last, regaling them with your fascinating stories about the crazy-hideous time you've just had ONLY if genuinely asked. Keep in mind the line from the 1988 comedy-drama *Beaches*, when Bette Midler's character C.C. says: 'But enough about me, let's talk about you. What do you think of me?'

Sarah Nelson Smith

INVEST IN SOCIAL GOOD

No man is an island, entire of itself; every man is a piece of the continent, a part of the main.

– John Donne, *Devotions upon Emergent Occasions*

Our basic need for food, water, shelter and safety will, if met, ensure we remain alive. Add in decent quality sleep, the opportunity to learn and grow, and the love of family or friends, and we'll have pretty good prospects of remaining physically healthy. But to be truly happy, we need more.

Humans are fundamentally social creatures. We need to belong to social groups and to form meaningful relationships. We are motivated by the desire to be wanted, needed and to have people in our lives upon whom we can rely. We need to feel that we are a part of society, perhaps cheering on our team at a sports match, whether in the stadium or in the pub with friends and fellow supporters, posting photographs and comments on social media, so that they can gain the approval or 'likes' of our peers, and taking our children to scouts and judo and gymnastics and rugby club, so that they too can start learning how to build wider relationships, and how to carve out their own place in society.

Getting it right – developing the human connections that we crave – improves our health and wellbeing, and gives us higher self-esteem. We become more empathetic, more trusting and, as a consequence, others are more open to trusting and cooperating with us. Thus the positive feedback loop of social, emotional and physical wellbeing is set. We become better people, and we help others to become better people too. The converse is also true: a lack of social connection is a greater knock to our health than obesity, smoking or high blood pressure, and can, in turn, lead to further isolation.

The role that we play within our societies is therefore key to determining how we feel about and in ourselves. Despite this, many of us massively underestimate it. There is plenty of low-hanging fruit easily within our grasp: many opportunities to improve both your own life, and the lives of others who will benefit from having you in their world. Make and nurture your connections with society. There is infinite opportunity to do good if you choose to do so, yet it's easy to be blind to the unique good that you can offer to others.

DO GOOD

> Do your little bit of good where you are; it's those little bits of good put together that overwhelm the world.
> – Archbishop Desmond Tutu

Whether or not you believe you have any specific skills, the knowledge and experience that seem obvious or basic to you will be new and eye-opening to somebody who has not walked along the same path. Here are just a few suggestions (you'll find contact details for some relevant organisations in the Useful Addresses section at the back of the book); with a bit of imagination and research, you will discover many other ways to contribute your skills and experience to others.

Donate time

- Befriend and visit the elderly within the community.
- Walk dogs and care for pets at animal shelters.
- Listen to children reading in schools.
- Collect or sort donations to charity.

Donate experience

- Become a mentor to kids in schools or young people coming out of care.

- Become a business mentor to someone in your own or any other business.

- Sit as a trustee for a charity or school.

- Help people with CV writing or interview practice.

Something further afield

- When you go on holiday to developing countries, take an extra bag filled with shoes, pencils, writing paper, wooden toys and games to donate to local schools or orphanages.

- Volunteer in projects overseas.

Create something new

- Think about what truly matters to you: where would you like to give the help that might make the world of difference? What could you do to make that vision a reality?

These are just a handful of suggestions. Go Google more; ask Siri; ask Alexa; browse MeetUp: the options are endless! Meet people who share interests with you. Spend time with people who are very different from you and have had entirely different experiences, for whom you are 'the other'. Start to understand what matters to them enormously, and what simply doesn't trouble them, despite mattering a great deal to you. Bit by bit, you'll start to reassess whether the things that keep you awake at night are actually quite as significant as you perceive them to be. And you may find insights that help you to resolve or better cope with your own challenges. You'll better understand your place in the world: not quite as great a spot as some, but infinitely better than that occupied by many, and wonderfully, uniquely yours.

Sal's Shoes

My friend CJ realised that millions of children in the world have no shoes, making them extremely vulnerable to infection and injury, which is often left untreated. Without shoes, many children are not permitted to attend school.

Starting with a single parcel of her son Sal's outgrown shoes, carefully packaged and sent out to a friend in Zambia to distribute, CJ continued to collect more outgrown children's shoes from family and friends. Sal's Shoes was born.

Word spread and soon CJ was inundated with pairs of barely worn shoes. That first year, she collected 4,805 pairs of shoes and distributed them in eight countries, including in the UK. Five years later, she gently fitted the millionth pair of shoes on the feet of their new owner (www.salsshoes.com).

In what ways could you follow in her footsteps and use your own insights and passion to help make the world a better place?

LIVING EACH DAY

I described elements of the beginning and middle of my trip through Latin America in Chapters 1 and 3. The end of the experience, however, found me being tossed mercilessly by the waves in a Mexican seaside surfers' paradise called Puerto Escondido.

At least, I have it on very good authority that it is a surfers' paradise. From my own limited experience of the place, there was no riot of colourful beach towels and parasols peppering the shore, while coffee-skinned children hopped between them, trying to avoid burning their feet on the scorching sand. There were no handmade leather bracelets being touted, nor offers of beaded hair braids, for a price, and there was no ice-cream vendor to be found. The beach was deserted. The peak season had either passed before our arrival, or had yet to begin. What remained were towering, angry waves crashing relentlessly onto the shore as Fannie, John and I stood, gazing out to sea, sizing them up with some trepidation. That we decided to shed our clothes and launch ourselves into the water was not the natural consequence of our ability to correctly assess the relative risks and merits of doing so, given the strong undercurrent and our lack of knowledge of the area. No, it was simply that we'd had another long bus journey, and we were all tired and hot. So in we went.

Getting in wasn't any sort of difficult, nor was swimming towards the mounting swell of each wave, then being held aloft by it, or diving just below its crest like dolphins, depending on what our nerve allowed. No, the difficulty didn't really become apparent until we tried to get out again. No matter how hard we swam towards the shore, our every sinew invested in the effort to escape from the water, we were pulled again and again back into the deep by the sea's infinite, impossible strength.

We had become separated, John, Fannie and me, and after some time, I spotted the two of them: Fannie was cast exhausted onto the eventual safety of the sand, heaving deep grateful breaths. And John, standing looking anxiously out to sea, was trying to find my face amongst the white seahorses that charged towards him. It struck me, then, that there would only be two possible exits: (i) right here and right now, somehow; or (ii) at some later date, when my dental records would prove more relevant than they had ever been before.

I faced John and Fannie and, with a final gulp of air, forced myself down, below the top current. And I kicked like hell. My arms and legs pummelling against the tide, I dragged myself through the water towards the beach. Every few seconds, the pull of a wave would summon me closer towards the surface and away from the shore, but still I swam. Almost out of breath, I needed to surface. But which way was up? With neither gravity nor daylight penetrating through the water to guide me, I had no idea. It's unsettling to realise that, whilst you are investing every dwindling iota of energy and strength in trying to survive, you have perilously low odds of even being pointed in the right direction.

I continued to kick. Swift as a gritty sucker punch to the ribs, I felt the sea bed smack against my side, pulling at my bikini and tearing my skin. Any hope or pretence of control over my own body now gone, I cartwheeled and tumbled, knees over chin over heels over skull – my hair inseparable from the sand, the water inseparable from my breath, my fingernails clawing at sand then water then finally, miraculously, at nothing at all.

Through the sand and water that filled my ears, I heard John, leaning over me, shouting my name, as the sea edged away, acknowledging at last that its game had come to an end. For some time, I did nothing but be alive, and spit up sand and sea water that filled my mouth and hid frustratingly underneath my tongue. My eyelids scratched what they sought to protect as they opened. Hot blood coursed down from my hip, disappearing into the sand beneath me. My hair, a matted sandy net covering my face. I pulled it aside and squinted up at a hot grey sky. 'Another day!' I congratulated myself, grinning. 'I get to live another day!'

CHOOSE YOUR FUTURE: BE BRAVE, BE HONEST

There are moments in life that cause us to pause, take stock and reassess, such as a great success or failure – or a sudden or eventual ennui with the tedium that we have allowed to engulf us. Such moments are rare gifts, and should be treated as such. Fear of the unknown and comfort with the present are equally inhibitive of great change and growth. But what if that comfortable stability were to be rocked, weakening the pull to remain, and making the unknown seem attractive for the potential that it offers?

Preparing for, experiencing and clawing your way out to the other side of a crisis can be a time of adrenaline and drama; of seeing the best and worst in people; of failing fast and learning urgently and realising, as the crashing waves recede, that not only have you survived the experience, but that you are stronger and wiser as a result. The landscape may have shifted, but so too has your perspective of it. And that feeling in the pit of your stomach – the ache that throbbed upon waking and upon remembering, tormenting you as you tried to make the wisest decisions and take the bravest actions: it is gone. After the joy of its departure has settled though, you may realise that it was significant enough to have left behind it a void. Now it is your choice how to fill this void.

Don't waste the momentum that has brought you through to this moment. Of course, allow yourself to recover and to regain your equilibrium, but before life has calmed entirely, think actively. Question intrusively. Deciding to make no change may well be the right path for you. But it might not: now that your eyes have been opened, what else might be possible?

What else might bring you all that you seek, but that perhaps you hadn't contemplated before?

I challenge you to challenge yourself.

HOW AM I REALLY... ?

Make time and space to think clearly and honestly. This may be the moment to return to your hygge, or to take yourself somewhere quite removed from everyday life. If you're better at thinking things through when you have someone to debate and discuss with, turn to your tribe and ask for a sounding board to help you out.

Whatever works for you, you deserve this: you deserve to seize the opportunity to choose your own future, rather than to stumble blindly and thoughtlessly into it, with no say over what it might contain. You spend time choosing a holiday, a car, new wallpaper, or a new home to live in, each decision sufficiently important to take up hours, days, even months trawling the internet and asking friends and family for their thoughts (okay, perhaps not about the wallpaper). Your future matters more than these things.

Are you completely satisfied with your present?

- Don't restrict yourself to considering only things that you think are rectifiable, while ignoring other issues, e.g. *I hate the commute, but wherever I work, I'd have to commute, so there's no point in mentioning it.* No: if it is a dissatisfier, list it.

- Have you got the balance of excitement and calm, challenge and comfort, just right? Do you have sufficient opportunity to continue to grow and develop? Have the rose-tinted glasses cracked and revealed imperfections that had previously lain hidden?

- Recognise the new truth and be true to that: what might have been perfect then is not necessarily the right fit for now. This need not be categorised as a good thing or a bad thing: it simply is what it is.

If you are not satisfied now, what is it that you're looking for?

- It is often not the thing you think it is: you might believe that *a more senior job title* would give you greater satisfaction, but in reality, it's pretty meaningless. Are you instead looking for recognition for having done something fantastic? Do you simply want to feel valued and appreciated? A job title or pay increase will not necessarily give you that.

- It might be more insightful to work backwards: don't think about what tangible things you want, but instead, consider how you want to feel. Then, imagine the possible paths that could get you there.

If you could change anything about your situation, what would it be?

- Do not be constrained by what you *know* to be possible: think instead to what you *wish* were possible and work backwards. Might some elements of it be achievable? Or perhaps a completely different and innovative route will get you to this (or a better!) destination?

What is preventing you from making this change now?

- Look back to Chapters 2 and 3, and remember how to

discern what you need, and how to get your brave on to achieve it. Might this be a Bucket 2 scenario? ('The worst case scenario is not quite as apocalyptic as it might seem: you will survive. You should do it.')?

> What scares you more: the thought of everything changing forever, or the thought of nothing changing ever?

I remember seeing a miserable looking guy in a tired, faded black suit on the tube: he stood, inert, unseeing eyes staring at nothing at all, with a round red badge pinned to his black knitted scarf the only colour in his outfit. It read: 'Wage Slave'. I got off at the next stop, thinking, please, let that never be me.

The best time to plant a tree was twenty years ago. The second best time is now.
– Chinese proverb

13. Keep Your Promises

Sitting one evening in the office with Lawrence and Rachael, two lovely members of my team and work tribe, Lawrence asked me, 'Will there be a chapter about me in your book?'

Rachael and I laughed, perhaps a little too much, at the question.

'Of course!' I assured him, smiling.

*

'And will your book be dedicated to us, Mum?' Mattie and Jossie asked me each night, as I tucked them in and told them that yes, I would be heading back downstairs to write. 'Will it have our names written in the front?'

'Yes,' I whispered, turning out the light. 'Of course it will.'

KEY LEARNING

Keep your promises: they might mean more to the people to whom you make them than you realise.

Epilogue

At the time of writing this epilogue, it is exactly a year since the KFC distribution crisis erupted, against the stark backdrop of a sudden deep winter. It is a year since I, and many others, seized the Bucket 2 scenario, and put everything and everyone else on hold in order to try to wrestle that particular beast back into submission, and the chicken and chips back into the restaurants.

Change is a welcome – if not always an inevitable – consequence of turbulence. Impossibilities suddenly appear to be options, and 'facts' reveal themselves as the opinions they really are. The fear of what life might look like if everything changes fades into a new fear of what life might be like if *nothing* changes.

It was suddenly very clear to me: I was ready for change. The idea of leaving a company and a job that I loved had not previously seemed to me a possibility, let alone a priority. I hadn't given serious thought to starting in a new role, with new challenges, since arriving at KFC. Now, though, having travelled with the company through incredibly turbulent waters and emerged exhausted but still smiling on the other side, I began to question what other challenges might be awaiting me elsewhere. With serendipitous timing, I received an invitation to consider a new role within a fast-growing new company called WeWork. There would be mountains to climb, and numerous challenges and pitfalls along the way, I was cautioned by the recruiter. I smiled to myself: in that case, count me in.

*

Cycling into my new office in London this morning, I crested the first and largest hill on my journey. I paused to unzip my jacket and take in the watercolour image of London, cradled in the distance as the thick fog gave way to a beautiful liquid sunrise. The unlit country road ahead would soon merge with another; a roundabout would knit two A-roads together, and within an hour, my solitary course would be taken over by a swarm of cyclists, growing in number from side roads and driveways as the distance to the city fell away.

'New bike?' a familiar stranger asked me as we paused, the commuter peloton clustered at the front of the snake of traffic, eager for the lights to change.

I had bought it the previous week. My treasured early morning workouts with Paul and the team had sadly fallen by the wayside as they proved incompatible with my new commute. A few weeks into my new job, I realised that if I couldn't join the classes any more, I would need to figure out a Plan B. Time to myself would be in short supply, so instead of fitting training in around my commute, it would need to become my commute.

One junction on: 'Yes!' my reply. 'First week on it!'

An approving nod. 'Enjoy the ride!'

The lights flicked to green, and in a surge of Lycra and flashing red lights, we were gone.

'Oh, I will,' I thought to myself. 'I'm certain of that.'

*

All unstable states must end. The lucky streak; the downwards spiral; the state of confusion; the honeymoon period; the period of crisis. The vertiginous highs and the stomach-churning lows will even out and, in their wake, will be quiet plateaus, hard-won experience and a new perspective on the world. We are all impacted by our experiences in one way or another. The bullied might become the bully or might instead become the champion of the underdog, the friend to those in need. The person scarred by failure might tread the most cautious of paths in the future, avoiding all possible risk; or he might take from the experience the knowledge that he can survive even those situations that terrify him, and emerge stronger as a result.

You must choose how your next chapter will begin. Decide what impact you will allow your experiences to have on you. Take the time to understand yourself, your needs, and your new circumstances, then choose to navigate them with courage and with positivity. Allow your tribe, whether longstanding or newly assembled, to help you along the way, and communicate clearly and openly as you go.

But don't forget, what now seems obvious to you may still be a mystery to those who have trodden a different path. When there's an opportunity to share your story and give somebody a helping hand with theirs, don't be the one who forgets to mention the piranhas.

You have survived the knocks and blows that life has tested you with so far, and ridden the waves. You and I might never have met, but I believe in you.

You've got this.

Notes

CHAPTER 1. FIGURING IT OUT

1. Shakespeare, *As You Like It*, Act 3, Scene 2.

2. https://www.dove.com/us/en/stories/campaigns/ real-beauty-sketches.html

CHAPTER 2. UNDERSTANDING YOUR COMFORT ZONE

1. Jeppe Trolle Linnet, *Interweavings – A cultural phenomenology of everyday consumption and social atmosphere within Danish middle–class families*, 2010.

2. See http://hyggehouse.com/hygge

3. Quoted in 'Everybody's Free (To Wear Sunscreen)' by Baz Luhrmann, the lyrics of which are based on an essay by *Chicago Tribune* journalist Mary Schmich.

4. Speech at WeWork World Summit 2019, Los Angeles.

CHAPTER 3. GET YOUR BRAVE ON

1. Known as 'hysterical strength', a burst of extreme strength far in excess of what the person exhibiting it can ordinarily achieve. Most reported instances occur when a person, particularly a loved one, is in a life-and-death situation, and the 'victim' or the 'rescuer' is conscious that this is the only opportunity to ensure survival.

2. 'Teen Leaps Off Train Platform and Saves Toddler From Tracks in Milan', NBC News, 15 February 2018: An eighteen year old appeared to give no thought to his own safety as he jumped off the platform to rescue a two-year-old boy who had climbed onto the tracks. (https://www.youtube.com/watch?v=Pds6v_ITWrQ)

3. I'd love to take the credit for this phrase, but I first read it on a mug that I bought on a family holiday in La Rochelle in the 1990s. It can be attributed to many.

4. Commonly attributed to A. A. Milne, but in fact a quotation from the 1997 Disney film *Pooh's Grand Adventure: The Search for Christopher Robin*.

CHAPTER 4. FIND A ROLE YOU LOVE

1. The Magic Circle law firms are five global firms considered to be amongst the most prestigious in the world. Their elite status is based on factors including their client base, revenue per lawyer, revenue per partner and the number of lawyers that they employ.

CHAPTER 5. FIND YOUR TRIBE

1. See apps such as Meetup and Bumble BFF for ways to meet like-minded local people.

2. www.parkrun.org.uk – free, weekly, 5km timed runs in locations all around the world, open to everyone.

3. www.greatoutdoorfitness.com and similar websites offer outdoor training classes in East Surrey to cater for all abilities. A quick search on Google will turn up similar classes close to you.

4. In my case, Paul at www.greatoutdoorfitness.com

CHAPTER 6. UNDERSTAND THE BACKGROUND

1. For more information, see www.dpdhl.com/en/media-relations/press-releases.html

2. Quoted in 'KFC's UK chicken run caused by too many eggs in one basket', *Financial Times*, 23 February 2018.

CHAPTER 10. RECOGNISE THAT YOU ARE HUMAN

1. See https://www.thelordmayorsappeal.org/a-healthy-city/this-is-me/

2. For the names of some helpful organisations, see Useful Addresses.

CHAPTER 11. LEARN!

1. This model was originally developed in the 1960s, by Elisabeth Kübler-Ross, identifying the various stages of the griev-

ing process. It has since been widely adopted for use in change management coaching.

CHAPTER 12. KNOW WHEN TO WALK AWAY

1. Emma M. Seppälä PhD, 'Connect To Thrive: Social Connection Improves Health, Well-Being & Longevity', *Psychology Today*, 26 August 2012 (www.psychologytoday.com/gb/blog/feeling-it/201208/connect-thrive)

Useful Addresses

If this book has inspired you to find your own way of reconnecting and giving back to your community and society, here are some ideas to get you started. Alternatively, some of the organisations mentioned here might provide helpful resources in times of need.

UNITED KINGDOM

Age UK (www.ageuk.org.uk/get-involved/volunteer/community-befriender)

A charity that exists to help older people, providing vital support, information and advice, and helping to tackle issues such as loneliness.

Blue Cross (www.bluecross.org.uk/volunteer)

An animal charity helping sick, injured and homeless pets since 1897.

Do-it (www.do-it.org)

A digital charity supporting civil society, and a great resource for volunteering opportunities.

Family Action (www.family-action.org.uk/get-involved/ volunteer).

Aims to provide services and financial support which will strengthen and improve the life chances of those who are poor, disadvantaged or socially isolated.

Guide Dogs (www.guidedogs.org.uk)

Provides life-changing services for the independence of people living with sight loss and their friends and families. The incredible trained guide dogs are at the heart of the organisation. There are many opportunities for volunteers to support.

Mental Health First Aid (mhfaengland.org/)

Aims to normalise society's attitudes and behaviours around mental health, by developing the skills we need to look after our own and others' wellbeing.

NACRO (www.nacro.org.uk/)

A national charity that delivers social justice by positively changing lives, strengthening communities and preventing crime. There are many opportunities to get involved and support across England and Wales.

NCVO100 (www.ncvo.org.uk/ncvo-volunteering/i-want-to-volunteer)

A charity that champions the voluntary sector by connecting, representing and supporting voluntary organisations.

NHS Blood Donation (my.blood.co.uk)

Register to be a blood donor, give blood and save lives.

OLIO (olioex.com)

OLIO is an app-based social enterprise, that connects neighbours with each other and with local businesses so surplus food (and non-food household items) can be shared, not thrown away. Opportunities to get involved begin with simply offering or accepting food, right up to helping to build new food-sharing communities in your area.

Sal's Shoes (www.salsshoes.com)

Crossing continents to make sure that your used, loved (and barely worn) outgrown children's shoes are delivered straight from you to those in need. Donate shoes or funds, or offer to spend a day shoe sorting and packing with the team.

Salvation Army (www.salvationarmy.org.uk/volunteering)

A charity that aims to help transform lives, working with some of the most disadvantaged people in our communities, including homeless people, older people, unemployed people, those suffering from drug and alcohol addiction, as well as victims of human trafficking and major emergencies.

The Samaritans (www.samaritans.org)

Working together to make sure fewer people die by suicide, and to make sure there's always someone there for anyone who needs someone.

The Sleep School (thesleepschool.org)

The UK's leading sleep expert, helping businesses and their employees, private individuals and parents to improve the quality of their sleep.

Trustees Week (www.trusteesweek.org)

Organises an annual event to showcase the great work that trustees do and to highlight opportunities for people from all walks of life to get involved in organisations as trustees.

VSO (www.vsointernational.org)

Brings people from different backgrounds, with a range of experiences and expertise, together to fight poverty around the world.

UNITED STATES

Big Brothers Big Sisters of America (www.bbbs.org)

Mentors work one-to-one with children, helping them improve their study habits, develop confidence, and learn to relate to adults.

Boys and Girls Club of America (www.bgca.org/get-involved/volunteer)

To enable all young people, especially those most in need

of support, to reach their full potential as productive, caring, responsible citizens.

Guide Dog Foundation (www.guidedog.org/Default.aspx)

A non-profit providing guide dogs to the visually impaired, and offering volunteering opportunities to walk dogs or raise puppies on behalf of the Foundation.

No Kid Hungry (www.nokidhungry.org)

Aims to end childhood hunger across the country by making sure all kids get nutritious food.

Shoes That Fit (www.shoesthatfit.org)

Helps children attend school in comfort – and with dignity – by giving them shoes to wear.

AUSTRALIA

Australian Red Cross (www.redcross.org.au)

Saving lives and supporting people before and after disasters strike. Also working to alleviate suffering during conflict and to assist the most vulnerable community members – no matter what their circumstances.

Fitted for work (fittedforwork.org/)

Helping people to dress appropriately for job interviews, providing advice regarding job interviews, writing application letters, mock interviews etc, and providing advice to help set them up for success, with guidance in writing application letters, mock interviews and plenty of encouragement.

Our Big Kitchen (www.obk.org.au)

A community run, non-denominational, industrial kitchen where meals are prepared for distribution to needy people across Sydney.

The Smith Family (www.thesmithfamily.com.au)

Helping disadvantaged Australian children to get the most out of their education, so they can create better futures for themselves.

Wrap with Love (www.wrapwithlove.org)

Provides warm wraps to help vulnerable people ward off hypothermia in Australia and over seventy-five other countries, with the help of hardworking and generous volunteers.

Other opportunities to volunteer:

- www.australiancharityguide.org/find-a-charity
- govolunteer.com.au
- www.volunteer.com.au

(None of the listings implies an endorsement by or of the named organisation.)

Acknowledgements

I'd like to say a huge and very heartfelt thank you to my tribe. Many of you have peppered the pages of this book with your wisdom, truth and encouragement, but the reality goes so much further than these pages could possibly capture. You mean the world to me.

First (individual) thank you must go to my brilliant and inspirational friend Camilla: if it weren't for your unwavering belief and 24/7 encouragement, beginning over a peculiar meal in our local pub, and not ending yet, this book might yet be a 'one day' thought in my mind. Everyone needs a friend like you.

To my early readers and honest editors – Charles, Claire, Jen, Adam, Max, Lea, David, Nikki and my wonderful Mum: thank you for reading, discussing, advising and laughing at some of the particularly ridiculous bits that thankfully didn't make it through to this final copy.

To Sue Lascelles, Mary Chesshyre and Andrew Chapman – thank you for helping to make this real: your thoughtful and insightful editing has nudged this into being a better and clearer expression of the story I really wanted to tell. Thank you for reading it, understanding it and partnering with me to share it. It has been a joy.

To Josh Hara – my incredibly talented, fun and accommodating illustrator. I'm delighted and honoured that you stepped away from the #100CoffeeCups for a while and supported me with this. Your artwork makes me smile a lot!

To my fantastic husband Adam, and incredible little girls – thank you for putting up with my antisocial hours and absences, whether due to the demands of work or writing. Whether I'm ensconced in an office, hidden away somewhere silently typing or wandering the giant chillers of a distribution centre in Rugby in the early hours of the morning, my heart is always wherever you three are.

To my fabulous friend Fannie: I treasure the time that we spent travelling together as students, hitch-hiking when our money ran out, and haggling by topping up funds with a song, with improbable success. I am glad to take your words as the title for this book. To me, the piranhas stand for the truth that is incredibly obvious to some, but a complete mystery to others who do not have the benefit of the same journey or experience. May we all be generous with others who might follow in our footsteps, and may we always seek to help them out by gently mentioning the piranhas.

Unbound is the world's first crowdfunding publisher, established in 2011.

We believe that wonderful things can happen when you clear a path for people who share a passion. That's why we've built a platform that brings together readers and authors to crowdfund books they believe in – and give fresh ideas that don't fit the traditional mould the chance they deserve.

This book is in your hands because readers made it possible. Everyone who pledged their support is listed below. Join them by visiting unbound.com and supporting a book today.

Raja Adil
Maria Alsabti
Suzanne Anderson
Becky Annison
Angela Antoniou
Steve Ash
Kashif Baig
Jonathan Baker

Natalia Baldizzoni
Kriztianne Baptista
Sian Bartle
Katherine Bellau
Fannie Bercez
Adrienne Berkes
Noelle Berryman
Lauren Bissell

Peter Blockley
Oleg Bodiul
Nick Bolter
Rob Booth
CJ Bowry
Kato Bowskill
Clare Boynton
Abby Bryon
Love Cake, Swanage
Chris Canham
Susana Cao Miranda
Elaine Carnegie
Nick Carnes
Gerard Carolan
Carmel Carroll
Queenie Chan
Clair Chapman
Frances Coats
Winsor Communications
Lisa Cornell
John Croft
Louisa de Jong
Daniel Deacon
Claire Deeble
Jo Dillon
Sarah Dixon
Simon Edwards
Nathalie Eida
Louise Eldridge
Louise Elliott Neal
Georgina Ellison
Anne Ellison
John Ellison
Anne Ellison
Marta Embid
Courtney Ferri
Rob & Aly Foyle
Charles Fromage
Chris Gallon
Zaid Gardner
Luke Govier
Hannah Graydon
The Green Rooms, Godstone
Kim Gundlach
Lucie Hammerton
Joshua Hara

Alison Hardy
Jennifer Hartzler
Jamie Henderson
Louise Hennessey
Jens Hofma
Roisin Holden
Linda Holland
Annette Hosler
Alice Ivanoff
Kristel Jarvis
Paul Jayson
Hilary Jones
Sacha Kakad
Roy Keldie
Emma Kennedy
Naveen Khela
Dan Kieran
Charlie Knight
Lea Korte
Esther Kwon
Christine Lamont
Max Lang
David Lavelle
Hayley Leake
Frieda Levycky
Clair Lissaman
Rhona Luithle
Emily Lyle
Krupa Madhvani
Eve Marlow
Mary Beth Martinez
Silvia Mazzone
Ann McDonnell
Mark Mear
Elisabeth Milan
John Mitchinson
Aaron Moore-Saxton
Juthamard Morgan
Nina Morgenstern
Hayley Murfin
Breda Naciri
Sarit Nathan
Carlo Navato
Paula Nelson
Kevin Offer
Laura Ottley

Samantha Partridge
Hannah Platts
Henk Pleiter
Justin Pollard
Daniel Porter
Gaby Prior
Paul Prothero
Mathieu Proust
Helen Puntha
Jo Rawlinson
Jamima Rey
Simon Robson
Krysia Rollinson
Ronnie Lin
Sue Roper
Susan Samuel
Giovanna Sessi-Knott
Gareth Shackleton
Kelly Shipsey
Spencer Shubert
Adam Smith
Jenny Smith
Robert Smith
Maggy Smith
Bill Southwell
Jill Southwell

Mollie Stoker
Gretchen Sutton
Maria Swift
Katie Taylor
Laura Terrell
Sonia Thomas
Louise Trayhurn
Marsh Vaader
Michelle van Huyssteen
Vanessa Velasco
Rhea Vernon
Katie Vickery
Lola Von Runkel
Vonnie
Claire Wallingford
John Wallingford
Susan Wallingford
James Wallingford
Ross Wallingford
Clare Wardle
Robert Welbourn
Winner Winner Chicken Dinner
Karen Wood
Angela Young
Gabriella Ziccarelli